COMMONSENSE MANUFACTURING MANAGEMENT

COMMONSENSE MANUFACTURING MANAGEMENT

Excellence From the Shop Floor to the Executive Suite

John S. Rydz

1817

Harper & Row, Publishers, New York

BALLINGER DIVISION

Grand Rapids, Philadelphia, St. Louis, San Francisco
London, Singapore, Sydney, Tokyo, Toronto

International Standard Book Number: 0-88730-211-4

Library of Congress Catalog Card Number: 89-26708

Printed in the United States of America

Library of Congress Cataloging-in-Publication Data

Rydz, John S.

Commonsense manufacturing management: excellence from the shop floor to the executive suite / John S. Rydz.

   p.   cm.

   ISBN 0-88730-211-4

   1. Production management. I. Title.

TS155.R93   1990

658.5—dc20

658,5
R992

                                        89-26708

                                          CIP

To Clare,
whom I had the
common sense to marry

Contents

Preface

During the past five years I have witnessed a dramatic re-surgence of companies that are initiating programs which will help restore their manufacturing competitiveness. Au-tomation, computer-aided design, just-in-time, and statisti-cal process control, are some examples of the programs that are being conducted by U.S. manufacturing plants. More-over, company executives are once again devoting attention to their manufacturing operations.

Certainly, these developments are positive signs that U.S. companies are revitalizing their factories in order to produce higher quality products at less cost, as well as becoming more responsive to their customers' delivery schedules. All of these actions are major steps forward in comparison to manufacturing during the sixties and seventies. During that time period, the United States lost its long-held dominance in manufacturing.

Significantly, the century-old position of dominance held by U.S. manufacturing was successfully eroded by the prod-uct-and-process technologies of global competitors. When combined with lower labor costs, favorable currency rates, and barriers against U.S. trade, competitors were able to use technology and high-quality performance to destroy our edge. These countries often produced better quality products and provided equal or better delivery and service levels to the United States and other countries that were traditionally its international markets.

As we enter the nineties, we now have an opportunity to restore our manufacturing competitiveness. U.S. companies once again have an opportunity to take an innovative lead in competing in the global economy. The environment in the United States today promotes the restoration of manufacturing plants to their former position. A key question needs to be considered, however. Are manufacturing managers ready to respond to the challenge? My concern about the readiness of manufacturing managers to respond to the challenges of the nineties prompted me to write this book.

I believe that the true competitive advantage of the United States lies in its ability to create and apply new and innovative product and manufacturing technologies. If properly deployed, U.S. innovative potential could compensate for unfavorable labor rates and other barriers that continue to surface as it becomes a stronger global competitor.

My concern about manufacturing managers is based on years of fostering advanced technology for the manufacturing operations of Emhart Corporation. In some divisions that were encouraged by corporate management to upgrade their manufacturing operations we encountered opposition from management, labor, and even manufacturing engineers who preferred to continue with traditional manufacturing equipment or obsolete manufacturing processes. Those of us who helped move new technology into manufacturing during the seventies learned from disappointing experiences that ''old line'' manufacturing cultures were difficult to change. In some cases, change did not occur because of the rigid habits that pervaded the organization. Today, many of these divisions are facing especially tough competition from foreign competitors.

Even when changes do occur, managers will often implement programs hastily with minimal analysis or without understanding the overall implications of the changes. In many cases, the operating results are often disappointing since long-term expectations are not achieved. As an illustration, consider how some companies approached automation in the early seventies. Very little attention was given to the product being automated. Often, the product was originally designed for manual assembly and was subjected to automation components that could not reliably orient nor reliably feed the product parts. Attending to these parts in the early automation planning stages, plus redesigning the product for automation could have saved many systems that were considered unsuccessful because of less-than-expected results. To the financial executives this failure meant that the automation system did not achieve its target-hurdle rate, or payback. Furthermore, these types of automation systems were often discontinued after employees devoted countless hours and financial resources were expended. A common-sense, up-front analysis, and a "design for automation" plan could have prevented "downstream" headaches and disappointments.

Besides my manufacturing experiences, I also was encouraged to write this book by other manufacturing executives and members of academia who were conducting manufacturing research programs. All of us share the same opinion. Manufacturing managers must change the way they manage manufacturing in order to take full advantage of advanced technologies and information systems. Those of us who are responsible for fostering and encouraging the upgrading of manufacturing know that this improvement can only happen if manufacturing managers have a sense of vision. They are the future leaders who will be needed to create the changes that can take full advantage of emerging technologies. Thus, I believe that there is a need to reexamine how we manage manufacturing.

Apart from attempts by U. S. companies to revitalize their

own manufacturing competitiveness, several manufacturing programs are also being developed at the state and national levels. Within many states, manufacturing centers are being established with funding from both industry and government. The major objective of state governments is to encourage industry to keep its manufacturing operations within their borders. Thus many state governments are developing manufacturing center programs, as well as offering other incentives to industry in the hope of retaining manufacturing.

Many of these manufacturing centers are associated with a local university—usually its engineering school. Thus, in most centers the programs concentrate on applying technology to help solve the problems on the shop floor. In fact, most industrial members of the center encourage the "problem solving" approach. For this reason, the centers established in the seventies concentrated on technologies such as robotics, automation, computer-aided-engineering, and computer-aided manufacturing.

As a technologist, I certainly encourage implementing technology throughout all sectors of manufacturing. I also see a major need in many of these manufacturing centers, however. More effective management techniques to transfer technology from the university manufacturing center to industry must be developed. This is a key management area that needs attention throughout most manufacturing centers.

From an industry point of view, many executives and managers believe that sufficient technology has already been developed. These managers want to learn more about the technology, and most important, discover effective ways to integrate technology into their manufacturing operations. I strongly encourage those who are directing university manufacturing centers to include the management of technology as a major component of their manufacturing and academic programs.

At the national level, many government agencies are actively pursuing manufacturing programs through research initiatives. Among these is a major manufacturing research program conducted by the National Science Foundation (NSF). The major thrust of NSF is not only to foster the creation of new manufacturing technologies, but to develop innovative applications of technology in manufacturing. Significantly, NSF is pursuing manufacturing research as one of its major emphases. Part of this strategy entails calling on industry for input on future manufacturing research needs. This was the case in 1986, when NSF invited members from industry and academia to attend a manufacturing workshop.

On October 3, 1986 NSF conducted a Workshop on a Stategic Manufacturing Research Initiative in Washington, D.C. The workshop brought together twenty-six participants from industry, academia, and NSF. I was pleased to have been invited to this workshop, which brought together a group of people from industry and academia who are knowledgeable about the status of manufacturing and manufacturing research.

The objective for the workshop group was to recommend to NSF the components of a research strategy that enables U.S. manufacturing technology to move ahead in large jumps without having its advantage readily overcome by foreign competition. Two general concerns pervaded the meeting, namely: (1) the ability of the United States to compete globally is a serious national concern, especially for the nation's manufacturing industries, which appear particularly vulnerable to overseas competition; and (2) further reductions in U. S. manufacturing output threaten the nation's defense base and the entire engineering infrastructure which forms the nation's technological base.

The participants of the workshop concluded that the competitive advantage of the United States lies in its strong scientific and engineering base and that the engineering fields of design and manufacturing are ripe for revolutionary intellectual advances. The group also concluded that if these revolutionary design and manufacturing advances are managed skillfully, the United States could regain its distinction of being the world's greatest manufacturing nation.

I was especially pleased that the workshop group specifically identified the need to manage expertly new design and manufacturing advances. Throughout my close association with manufacturing I have continually seen the need to not only upgrade manufacturing management, but to also bring new management concepts into the field of manufacturing. Interestingly, I believe that many of these management concepts are not necessarily new, but often apply commonsense principles.

Perhaps some of these commonsense concepts are new to manufacturing managers who for many years were entrenched in traditional thought processes. This narrow view of manufacturing was fostered by a management that focused too much on the labor element of manufacturing cost and by executives who were strongly influenced by the short-term outlook that pervades many companies even today. Hopefully, *Commonsense Manufacturing Management* will help change many of the traditional thought patterns of manufacturing managers. I hope that managers and those aspiring to join the management ranks will enjoy this book just as I have enjoyed my technical management career.

Acknowledgments

I acknowledge with great appreciation the help and stimulating ideas that were given to me by my colleagues from industry, government, and academia. Throughout my business career I have been most fortunate to have been associated with so many interesting people. These valuable acquaintances not only made my business career interesting and exciting, but their thoughts and ideas provided me with many valuable insights which I continue to draw upon for the management of technology. I will not be able to thank them all, so I will mention only a few who have been most helpful in what has been a most exciting and rewarding experience for me in the management of technology.

From academia, I owe special thanks to Dean Wesley L. Harris, Professor James M. Utterback, Professor Robert T. Lund, Professor Nam P. Suh, Dean Donald N. Zwiep and Dean Lewis N. Walker. They not only provided many stimulating concepts through many hours of discussions, but also gave me the opportunity to meet with students as a lecturer and teacher.

From industry, the list is too long to include the many friends I made during my management career. However, let me list some of these special individuals who were a great help in implementing new approaches to manufacturing management—Wally Abel, Bill Cadogan, Dick Campbell, Dave Dandro, Ray De Vita, Don Genaro, Blake Humphrey, Gil O'Neil, Bill Lichtenfels, Peter Scott, Fred Hollfelder, Peter Clackson, Wally Werner, Charles Lamb, James Rudd, Bob Douglas, Ralph Seel, and many other business associates to whom I say many thanks.

From the National Science Foundation, I would like to thank the staff members who gave me the opportunity to better understand the cross-disciplinary concept that will be the wave of the future in academia, engineering, and manufacturing. Finally, a special thanks to my secretary, Claire De Joseph. How she kept order with my files and my schedule was indeed an innovative achievement.

COMMONSENSE
MANUFACTURING
MANAGEMENT

Introduction

Finally, after nearly twenty years of frustration and playing a defensive role, manufacturing now has the opportunity to take the offense. Yes, manufacturing can now carry the ball, score the points, and help win the game.

For over thirty-five years I have been associated with manufacturing companies. During most of this time, product development rather than manufacturing dominated corporate strategies. Manufacturing throughout the seventies and early eighties was at best on the defensive. More often it was something that management wanted to forget about and move offshore.

As we enter the nineties, attitudes toward manufacturing are turning around. Once again top executives are addressing manufacturing issues in their speeches. Manufacturing centers are being created in universities. Government agencies, such as the National Science Foundation (NSF), National Aeronautics and Space Administration (NASA), National Institute of Standards and Technology (NIST), and the Defense Advanced Research Projects Agency (DARPA) are focusing on manufacturing. State governments are establishing programs and initiatives to foster manufacturing competitiveness in their states. Most important, a manufacturing career can offer challenging opportunities for new graduates and engineers who select manufacturing as their career path.

The ball is now in manufacturing's court. And as we enter the nineties the question is whether manufacturing managers can take the initiative. Can manufacturing executives and managers and shop-floor leaders seize this opportunity and return manufacturing to a strategic position within their companies?

I believe that manufacturing can do it. The task, however, is not an easy one. Change on the shop floor will require major cultural shifts: Top management commitment must become even stronger; greater team work among all company functions must become a way of life. Above all, the vision and determination of managers must move manufacturing beyond the grimy, obsolescent position it held in the seventies and into a twenty-first century filled with exciting and challenging opportunities so that manufacturing can reclaim its position in the corporate hierarchy.

Why am I optimistic? First of all, I lived through the demise of manufacturing in the seventies, when top management turned its attention to mergers, acquisitions, cost cutting, restructuring, and takeovers. I survived through product development, yet I always believed that the innovative potential within manufacturing was tremendous. As management turned its attention toward other strategies, permanent damage occurred: Manufacturing personnel simply gave up. With no one listening, people simply accepted their factories turning out poor quality products. Life on the factory floor became one problem after another. High inventory covered poor quality and poor scheduling. In many factories employees simply put in their time.

Moreover, in the seventies technical personnel who could not cut it in product engineering ended up in manufacturing. Only occasionally would bright graduates enter manufacturing, and they soon left. Those few who remained managed to create some improvements but only with a great deal of perseverance.

Today, top management recognizes the need for change and is willing to make a strategic commitment to change. Manufacturing managers must grab the ball and run.

I have seen what can be accomplished. I want manufacturing to succeed and manufacturing personnel to become part of the winning team. Most important, I want manufacturing to be part of a company's competitive strategy.

Through this book, I hope to show managers that actions can be taken to restore manufacturing competitiveness. By applying commonsense approaches, managers can help manufacturing regain a strong strategic position within their companies.

Part 1 examines the environment existing in today's companies. It challenges the belief that manufacturing and service are taking the United States down two separate paths and examines how the combination of manufacturing and service can ultimately move manufacturing forward. It explores the reason why manufacturing lost its strategic edge and how manufacturing managers can become the agents of change.

Part 2 describes the factory of opportunity. Companies are instituting the changes necessary to create the factory of and for the future, and technology will help restore manufacturing competitiveness in a global economy. Manufacturing must think and act globally in order to cope with the international forces confronting U.S. companies now and increasingly in the future.

In Part 3, finance, external relationships, and human resources are examined as keys to implementing advanced technology. External changes are taking place that offer manufacturing the opportunity to join forces with other companies and universities to nurture new ideas and encourage innovation. This part explores the most important element of manufacturing that technologists need to address—human resources.

Finally, Part 4, explores how we can make what went wrong, go right. It identifies how infrastructures can be put in place to restore manufacturing as a successful strategy for the future. Manufacturing managers can apply its common-sense approaches to nurture the vision and implement the steps required to restore manufacturing to its leading position in the next century.

Part I

Manufacturing: A Change Is Needed

1

American Manufacturing Today

Running a factory in the United States these days is not an easy job. The corps of several thousand manufacturing managers—mostly men—works hard under difficult conditions and isn't much appreciated. Unlike their corporate colleagues, these managers don't lead exciting lives, jetting around the globe from deal to deal. They are tied to their factories almost every day of the year, and these factories are often unpleasant places to work. Their pay is relatively low compared to their corporate counterparts, and they have a hard time finding good people to work for them.

Their factories are constantly in crisis, and the managers take the blame for it. The Occupational Safety and Health Administration (OSHA) and the unions blame them for the factory's working conditions. The marketing and engineering departments blame them for consumer complaints about poor product quality. The Environmental Protection Agency denounces them for the company's environmental record. The corporate bosses blame them for high costs, stagnant productivity, and unrest in the labor force. And every day, the factory managers have to contend with new forces in the marketplace that they didn't have to think about ten or even five years ago, forces such as foreign competition and more demanding customers.

Management whizzes from the corporate office sweep through and try to sell them the latest panacea—some magical solution designed to transform the factory into a smoothly operating machine that will put Japanese and Korean competitors out of business. Sometimes the panacea is technological (computer-aided design, robotics, computer-aided manufacturing); sometimes it's a management technique (just-in-time, theory X, quality circles). But whatever ideas top management proposes, these managers have little alternative but to try them all, without first establishing whether they're appropriate for their plant.

Not surprisingly, these techniques are never miracle cures. Sometimes they help, and sometimes they make things worse. But most frustrating is the way they are tossed haphazardly down to the factories from the corporate suite— one after the other, with no overall plan for manufacturing in mind. This pattern makes painfully clear to manufacturing managers that other things are more important at the corporate office and that their plants are not part of the strategic plan for the company's success. In the end, manufacturing managers remain in stressful and unrewarding jobs, working under difficult conditions and often fighting a losing battle. Like many other factories, sooner or later theirs probably will be shut down and replaced with so-called offshore sourcing—plants in Asia or other parts of the Third World where low labor costs can make up for a multitude of other sins in the manufacturing process.

In most ways, the plight of each one of these thousands of manufacturing managers is a microcosm of U.S. manufacturing as a whole. New demands are changing the business environment in which manufacturing companies work. Almost every year global competition, financial pressures from management, demands of enlightened consumers, and stockholders, new forms of regulation, and increasing threats of litigation from product and environmental liability are countered with new panacea solutions, but our factories show little improvement.

Recently, U.S. manufacturing has had some good news. The number of manufacturing jobs has stabilized, and the foreign trade deficit has improved. These are welcome improvements, but they are only surface signs. The root causes of manufacturing decline in the United States still have not been addressed, and the overall decline has not been arrested.

A Bumpy Road: Today's Manufacturing Career Path

As anybody who has worked in manufacturing over the last thirty years knows, it wasn't always like this. In the glory days of U.S. economic prosperity after World War II, manufacturing was the most critical component of corporate success. The product was the center of U.S. corporate culture. The top companies were run by executives who cared about their products and made sure their organizations worked hard to create competitive new lines. But beginning in the sixties corporate America began to change. The product became less important as the bottom line became more important. A wave of mergers and acquisitions created large conglomerates run by financially oriented executives who were not rooted in any particular industry or product and who emphasized return on investment over staying on top of the market in any particular product field.

These new executives moved their corporations away from the internal development of new manufactured products and turned to other, less arduous methods of expanding markets. Many corporations simply acquired small companies, while others created new products cheaply by combining different pieces of existing technology: The clock/radio is an example of this sort of quick-and-dirty hybrid. As the development of new manufactured products became less important to U.S. corporations, the role of manufacturing waned.

Manufacturing is no longer the focus of most companies' business but is just one operational component. Confronted with foreign competition, many corporations don't respond by revamping their manufacturing operations here in the United States; they simply procure the entire product or parts from overseas, where labor is cheaper. The prevailing wisdom among executives at these corporations seems to be that a powerful in-house manufacturing operation isn't necessary today—that the marketing leverage of a large and established company means it can sustain long-term growth through these outsourcing strategies. Corporate critic Seymour Melman, author of *Profits without Production*, characterized this attitude this way: "If you move production offshore, you save all the headaches. You don't have to design production. You don't have to run it. All you do is market the product. And the financial analysts applaud."

Furthermore, as manufacturing has become a backwater in corporate America, it also has become a less attractive career choice for the talented people who might be able to arrest the decline. What graduate of a prestigious business school would pass up Wall Street, management consulting, or the corporate suite to toil in a factory? As Harvard business professor Wickham Skinner recently wrote in his book, *Manufacturing in the Corporate Strategy* (John Wiley & Sons, 1978),

> My talks with students indicate that factories still represent grease and sweat and unimportant trivia; the minutiae of a multitude of small details; and the confrontation with rough, uneducated people and a militant union. . . . Presumably missing is the glamour and breadth of exposure in marketing, the big-dollar deals in finance, and the precision and sense of the overall business felt in the field of control.

"Factories," Skinner's business students conclude, "are for engineers." Yet even talented young engineers don't see much future or excitement in manufacturing. They are far more interested in research and development, which offers more rewards in terms of both prestige and money.

This has created a Catch-22: The more manufacturing companies fail to capture good young minds, the more the sector declines; the more the sector declines, the more determined the best students, managers, and executives are to find some other line of work. Occasionally some company or small segment of the manufacturing sector manages to make a little headway in this discouraging environment, but it is not enough to counteract the overall impression that the U.S. manufacturing sector is dying.

I am no stranger to the plight of the manufacturing manager. Early in my career, I worked on the shop floor and witnessed its grievance procedures, its work stoppages and slowdowns, and its misunderstandings and lack of communication. Later, as a member of top corporate management, I lived through the shift of manufacturing from the United States to low-cost countries in the Third World. Now, as vice president of technology at Emhart Corporation, I am responsible for moving emerging technology into factories that have lost their competitiveness—factories in all sorts of industries, including glass-bottle machinery, appliance timers, rivets and adhesives, and electronic automation equipment.

Because of these experiences in manufacturing, I know what it's like to work as a manufacturing manager. I've seen the long-term consequences managers suffer because they must devote themselves to putting out fires. I've experienced the chaos that occurs at the end of every month, when monthly financial results require the shipping of everything that can possibly be shipped. I've shared the many pressures managers feel, both from the top of the organization and from the shop floor itself.

As a corporate executive for more than twenty years, I also know the pressures of the corporate suite. I have watched the stock price every day and tried to keep it up to avoid takeover attempts. I've performed show-and-tell presentations for institutional investors. I know what it is like to be overwhelmed by legal and environmental rules when you're trying to run a corporate division.

I know that there are many reasons for the decline in U.S. manufacturing, including often cited problems like out-moded capital plants and high labor costs, which sometimes are regarded as intractable. Yet I believe manufacturing can be restructured and thrive again in the United States.

I am not alone in this belief. Many academics and man-ufacturing advocates have begun to rediscover the advan-tages of U.S. manufacturing. But few of these optimists have pinpointed what I believe is the true reason for our decline—and thus they have overlooked the path back to prosperity.

Manufacturing in the United States is in trouble because of the attitudes of the people at the controls—both the man-ufacturing managers and their corporate executive bosses. Too often they persist in perpetuating obsolete manufactur-ing operations. Under the gun from all directions, manufac-turing managers just about make it through to the end of each month. Awash in financial figures, their corporate bosses concentrate on finding ways to cut factory costs.

Neither group seems to see what I regard as the two most important facts about manufacturing in the United States today: First, U.S. manufacturing *must* survive—not just to benefit corporations but to benefit the nation as well; and second, the changing global economy has created enough opportunities for me to believe that despite bad publicity U.S. manufacturing *can* survive—and even prosper.

Why U.S. Manufacturing Must Survive

The increasing awareness in the United States that manu-facturing is important to the national prosperity generally has resulted from a belief that the national economy should be balanced and that high-paying blue-collar jobs are nec-essary to maintain a healthy middle class. But there are deeper reasons why manufacturing must survive—and they are important not only to economists but also to the executives of every large corporation in the United States. First, our rapidly growing service economy is closely tied to our manufacturing power, and one cannot be healthy without the other. Second, manufacturing is the linchpin of an entire system of technological innovation, which the United States needs and wants to retain. And third, domestic manufacturing can and should be viewed as a potent economic weapon by the United States and its companies. Let's examine these three factors in more detail.

Symbiosis with Service

The rise of the service economy in the United States has given birth to a kind of survival-of-the-fittest myth that the service sector will win out over the manufacturing sector in the long run. The truth is that they are not in competition with each other. In fact, each needs the opportunities the other provides in order to thrive.

Recently, a three-year study sponsored by the National Academy of Engineering noted strong connections between the two sectors. The researchers pointed out, for example, that manufactured goods often derive their value from the services they provide. A computer diskette—a manufactured good—is valuable not because of its magnetic coding but because of the data or programs it stores. Perhaps the most significant conclusion of the NAE researchers was that manufacturing companies have a voracious appetite for services and service companies have a voracious appetite for manufactured goods.

Professional services, for example, can require a large quantity of manufactured goods, particularly high-tech goods. In fact, the NAE researchers found that, according to a study by Morgan Stanley and Company, information workers in the service sector now require a greater capital investment—particularly high-technology investment—than industrial workers. Furthermore, the U.S. Bureau of Labor Statistics has found that nearly half of the thirty most capital-intensive industries in the country are service industries.

Consider the example of the Planning Research Corporation, a subsidiary of Emhart, the company for whom I work. PRC is a manufacturer of information systems, but its largest contract is with a service organization—one of the largest service organizations in the world, the United States government. PRC currently has a nine-figure contract with the U.S. Patent and Trademark Office to automate the office's 200-year-old records system, which was set up by Thomas Jefferson. In this instance, a manufacturing company benefits tremendously from a service organization's need for high-technology investment.

In addition to the volume of manufactured goods it requires, the service industry holds two other, more subtle advantages as customer for manufacturing companies. First, as the NAE study pointed out, because technological advances require constant replacement of equipment, service companies often must invest even during recessions, creating a stable market for manufactured goods. Second, service companies often require customized products. These products must be manufactured in small numbers but still produced at a low unit cost. This demand encourages manufacturing companies to pursue a strategy called computer-integrated manufacturing—a system that permits customized products to be manufactured at the same unit cost and is one of the best competitive weapons the United States has against foreign competition.

By the same token, the manufacturing sector is perhaps the most important force underlying the spectacular rise of service businesses. Increasingly, industrial companies have found it more efficient to acquire services—legal, purchasing, financial, accounting, even engineering and design—by purchasing them externally. According to economists Stephen Cohen and John Zysman, authors of the book *Manufacturing*

Matters (Basic Books, 1987), services purchased by U.S. goods-producing companies make up no less than *one-quarter* of the U.S. gross national product.

These services are not limited to outside lawyers and accountants—professionals whose work is important but not intimately tied to the manufacturing process itself. Manufacturing companies purchase a broad array of outside professional services, some of which are central to their success. For example, AT&T has farmed out much of its most important industrial design work to an outside firm, Henry Dreyfuss Associates. And Dreyfuss has responded by designing some of AT&T's most important products, including the Trimline phone. Outside firms can bring a fresh approach to an industrial design problem—and because they are smaller, they sometimes can produce conceptual or working models much more rapidly than in-house designers. Quick product development time is more important than ever, and this rapid turnaround can greatly assist a company's profitability.

Beyond all this interaction, however, the line between the service and manufacturing sectors is blurring and may eventually disappear. "Indeed, in many cases products and services are interchangeable," James Brian Quin, Jordan J. Baruch, and Penny Cashman Paquette wrote in their December 1987 *Scientific American* article, "Technology in Services". "A home washing machine (a product) can substitute for the use of a laundromat (a service), a frozen dinner for a meal at a restaurant, or CAD/CAM software for additional production equipment."

In *Manufacturing Matters*, Stephen Cohen and John Zysman use the example of a new telephone system to illustrate the increasingly blurred line between the two sectors. Not long ago, they said, $50 million in capital was needed to develop electromechanical switches for the phone system, and 2,000 workers were needed to produce them. Only fifty production workers are needed to manufacture digital switches, but the development cost has risen to $1.5 billion.

Most of that money goes to pay the salaries of so-called service workers—systems engineers and programmers who are in fact intimately involved in the manufacture of products.

Similarly, as *Industry Week* noted early in 1987 in a special report entitled "America's New Economy," the classification of many companies as either manufacturing or service may be misleading. General Electric is an industrial power-house, but it owns, among other things, General Electric Credit Corporation, the investment banking firm of Kidder Peabody and Company, and as part of RCA the NBC television network. In fact, RCA has always exemplified the service-manufacturing link. In the forties and fifties, while we engineers at RCA were busy making technological improvements for television sets, its NBC subsidiary was helping to build the market for those sets by putting programs on the air that people wanted to watch.

As another example of how the growing service business in the United States and manufacturing can tie together, consider the case of the Hartford Steam Boiler Inspection and Insurance Company of Hartford, Connecticut, which maintains the largest inspection and engineering organization in the world. Hartford Steam Boiler offers insurance for property and equipment as well as a wide variety of engineering services. Its overall thrust, as quoted from their 1988 annual report is that "With careful inspection and sound underwriting, boiler accidents can be avoided." Their motto: "Allow us to inspect and we can insure."

Inspection and engineering services for insured property and equipment are indispensable for evaluating risk, helping prevent accidents, and controlling losses, and the company seeks to provide high quality technical and professional services that contribute to safety, reliability and efficiency.

Significantly, a recent acquisition, Radian Corporation, is a scientific research and consulting subsidiary based in Austin, Texas. Radian, as part of Hartford Steam Boiler, provides engineering and consulting capabilities to government and private industry. These services include environmental engineering, health and safety, material sciences, machinery diagnostics, pharmaceutical science, specialty chemicals, computer software systems, mechanical technologies, and technical service for the waste management industry. Many of these services are related to improving manufacturing operations.

Also within its engineering division based in Hartford, services are provided related to the fabrication of boilers, pressure vessels, and other kinds of equipment as well as quality assurance reviews, the application of acoustic emission technology, environmental testing, and training programs for owners and operators of power and production equipment.

Most important, Hartford Steam Boiler devotes considerable resources to developing and expanding the technical and engineering capabilities that help keep their customers' businesses operational. It employs a technical staff in excess of 2,000 people of whom more than 1,000 hold degrees in engineering, science, or other technical disciplines. Its strategy is to address the business concerns that customers face every day, and its technological developments touch issues ranging from the aging of the nation's production equipment to environmental protection.

Diverse advanced technologies like expert systems reliability engineering computer simulation, acoustics, and vibrational analysis software are not usually expected to be found in an insurance company. Yet these technologies exist at Hartford Steam Boiler, and in fact in many cases it represents a dominant position in technology leadership.

The aging of industrial equipment in the United States intensified in the mid-1970s, according to the Hartford Steam Boiler's 1988 annual report. High interest rates and overseas competition forced many companies to defer major capital expenditures for as long as possible, and postponing plans to replace older equipment (ranging from large turbine generators in utilities to small boilers) has resulted in machinery that is working harder and longer. The aging of America's equipment is important to Hartford Steam Boiler: According to their literature, the longer a machine operates, the greater the risk of breakdown, which can halt production.

It is interesting to note that Hartford Steam Boiler also developed artificial intelligence to help customers diagnose the condition of equipment like turbine generators and rotating machinery. TURBOMAC, a computerized expert system that is based on the expertise of turbo machinery specialists and duplicates their logic and thought process, is one of Hartford's AI programs.

Through TURBOMAC customers monitor their equipment while it is in service and measure or record symptoms such as unusual vibrations or other signs of impending problems. TURBOMAC diagnoses systems so that customers can make repairs or take other steps to prevent unnecessary down time and excessive wear on equipment.

In addition to using expert systems such as the TURBOMAC system, Hartford Steam Boiler is also concerned with reliability. It has invested substantial resources to developing and improving technologies that help diagnose equipment problems. The strategy is to provide customers with technology that has been well designed. The company uses finite element analysis to evaluate designs by modeling equipment under actual work conditions and pinpointing where the equipment might be vulnerable to stress.

A further example of how this insurance company is attacking problems in a way that will ultimately serve as a model for manufacturing companies as well is Hartford Steam Boiler's vibration monitoring program, a tool that gives customers vital information about their machinery. The program operates on the principle that a machine in proper operating condition should run smoothly and that vibrations are warnings of a potential problem. Using the sophisticated data acquisition system developed by company technologists, the program measures vibrations, thereby helping customers to evaluate equipment performance and monitor operating condition. With an analysis of what's happening on the production floor, a company can schedule maintenance more effectively and avoid expensive unplanned shutdowns.

These advanced technologies will help manufacturers, but they are being developed by an insurance company. Their immediate objective is to reduce the cost of customers' equipment failures, but the technologies that are being explored by Hartford Steam Boiler are advanced technologies that will ultimately expand across the manufacturing base of the United States.

I have seen firsthand the potential of many of these techniques to significantly improve the operation of machinery on the shop floor in manufacturing plants. When I was at the Singer Company, we jointly conducted a program with Richard Lyon, professor of acoustical engineering at the Massachusetts Institute of Technology, for monitoring industrial sewing machines for vibration and sound. Through this study we discovered that the electronic machine signatures could predict, in advance, the failures of bearings, "out of spec" conditions of mechanical linkages, as well as whether a shaft was rotating in a true condition.

These diagnostic technologies will ultimately provide manufacturing operations with the means to predict and schedule equipment maintenance and service and to monitor the capability of the machines to produce quality parts and hence eliminate inspection. Again, it is interesting to note that technology that will ultimately upgrade manufacturing plants is being pioneered by an insurance company.

These close ties between manufacturing and service must be strengthened. If they are not, the manufacturing opportunities created by the service economy—and the potential to expand the service economy by using the manufacturers as customers—will move beyond our borders.

Synergy with Engineering Research

Government and industry leaders in the United States have been concerned about the loss of manufacturing, but they have been assured that the U.S. system of technological innovation—which still leads the world—will remain dominant. After all, research and development, which is the backbone of technological innovation, depends on a highly educated work force and on the facilities of great universities—and no country can match the United States on either count. But we should not be smug.

When most people think of R&D, they think of basic research—pathbreaking pure scientific research conducted at leading universities such as MIT, Berkeley, and Stanford and at research facilities such as Bell Laboratories. This type of R&D often breaks new scientific ground, and leading scientists are rewarded with Nobel Prizes and other forms of recognition.

But another, equally important form of research is more closely tied to manufacturing competitiveness. Engineering research is the bridge between pure scientific research and the actual manufacture of products; it is, according to one definition, "the application of science in the creation of products and services."

Researchers take scientific breakthroughs and translate them into manufactured products we all can use. To use one example singled out by a recent Engineering Research Board report on the subject, "The evolution of the modern computer from electron tubes to transistors and then to integrated circuits is the result of engineering research that converted newly understood physical principles into practical working systems." Though R&D sometimes refers to basic research—particularly in a large corporation that has its own research labs—more often R&D is engineering research.

As the worldwide race to develop new products intensifies, the role of engineering research has grown. Companies that can quickly convert scientific breakthroughs into new products can outpace the competition. When companies from other nations look with envy at the way ideas are exchanged in Silicon Valley, they are not necessarily concerned with pure scientific research. Rather, they admire the fact that thousands of our brightest engineers work in one place, close to their factories, swapping ideas about how to make products better and how to create new products. The result has been the development of new products at astonishing speed.

Though many factories have left the United States, so far most engineering research has not. Thus, our widely admired system of technological innovation—scientific breakthroughs followed by practical application—remains intact. But if we don't retain a manufacturing base, we could lose our entire system of technological innovation.

Scientists conducting basic research need not locate close to manufacturing facilities because their scientific research is not directly connected to manufactured goods. But the engineers who turn scientific breakthroughs into new products cannot afford to be separated from their factories for very long.

When a manufacturing operation is cut off from its R&D operation, its own technology ultimately becomes inefficient, resulting in an overall decrease in productivity. At the same time, when R&D is cut off from the manufacturing operation, it loses touch with the real-world applications that lead to technological improvement and innovation.

Aggressive business development experts—especially those from ambitious, emerging nations like Korea—recognize this link. They know that if they can persuade companies to move factories into their country, sooner or later the engineers will follow. Thus, the disappearance of these manufacturing operations from the United States will ultimately mean the loss of a critical element of R&D—and the technological edge that Americans have long been proud of.

This is not just alarmist theory. This shift is happening. In recent years, Silicon Valley electronics firms, many of which were founded by Asian entrepreneurs, have been setting up engineering research shops in Taiwan and Singapore, and Asian countries are sprouting American-style industrial parks. Taiwan, in particular, has targeted Chinese electronics entrepreneurs operating in the United States and has established an office in Silicon Valley to lure them back home.

Other countries have recognized the need to acquire more sophisticated business operations. A few years ago, the Republic of Ireland tried to convince Emhart to build a glass-bottle equipment manufacturing plant in Dublin; we chose not to. More recently, however, Ireland asked us to locate an engineering facility there in hopes of retaining Irish engineers who are emigrating to other countries; this time around, the government didn't even ask about a manufacturing plant. Emhart is seriously considering Ireland's offer.

If engineering research continues to move overseas, the United States could relinquish some of its most outstanding opportunities. Recently, for example, American companies have made great strides toward replacing metals with newly engineered materials and composites, with a two-fold effect on technology. In some cases technologies are being developed to make existing metals processes more efficient, in order to stem the tide of these emerging new materials. These new technologies also are pointing the way toward new production techniques. New processing equipment as well as new instrumentation technologies, new materials-handling systems, and many new applications will have to be developed. New products will be produced that never would have been dreamed of with metals. The same will certainly be true of recent breakthroughs in superconductivity.

But what happens if these new products are manufactured overseas? The engineers responsible for improving these products and creating new ones will have to locate near the factories in order to stay in touch with the manufacturing operation, and this could mean the United States will lose these important engineering research operations. Ultimately, this means the United States will lose the edge in technological innovation associated with the fastest-growing sectors of the world economy. The subsequent output of these technological innovations—new process equipment and many new products—also will be lost to the U.S. economy.

The Strategic Value of Manufacturing

The final reason that U.S. manufacturing must survive is that, if properly used, it is perhaps the most potent competitive weapon this nation and its top corporations have. Financially oriented corporate executives often overlook this fact and view industrial operations merely in terms of cost to be reduced or even divested. But for many companies, the competitive edge lies in opportunities on the factory floor here in this country.

One example is Cypress Semiconductor Corporation in California. Cypress Semiconductor is a small firm with a highly paid work force. At first glance it seems to be a company that wouldn't stand a chance against the Japanese semiconductor giants. Yet Cypress is thriving because the company has used strategic opportunities in the manufacturing process to claim a competitive edge.

The traditional manufacturing company produced standardized products in huge quantities at a low unit cost. Today the giants of every industry still do. But many customers are demanding more customized and less standardized products, and Cypress has responded to that demand. The company manufactures seventy-one different kinds of semiconductors. By using manufacturing technologies, Cypress is able to produce special orders, short runs, and custom-designed items efficiently at little or no additional cost.

By using the manufacturing process as a competitive weapon, Cypress is able to be responsive to customer needs and neutralize the advantage of foreign competitors. And by finding ways to keep factories at home, companies such as

Cypress are also gaining an advantage over foreign competition in serving their American customers: They can provide better service simply because they are much closer.

As advanced technology progresses, manufacturing companies in the United States—large and small—will be presented with similar opportunities. Individually, these opportunities may not seem enormous, but together they create what I call the factory of opportunity.

2

How We Lost the Strategic Edge

Not long ago, Dynapert, an Emhart subsidiary, tried to discover causes of delay in product development in order to find ways to respond to customers more quickly. Dynapert is a leading supplier of automation equipment to the electronics industry, where quick customer response is essential. If a Dynapert customer is developing a new product for the consumer electronics market, that customer's manufacturing and marketing plans rest on Dynapert's ability to deliver new capital equipment by a specific date. To increase Dynapert's response rate, the company commissioned a study of the matter.

One of the things Emhart discovered was that Dynapert, like many other companies, develops new products in a serial manner—by completing one step before the next step is begun, perhaps by a different group within the company. For example, in the production of prototypes, product development groups finished the entire design before they began to build the models.

This serialization wasn't necessary, of course, because most parts used in the prototype were standard or proven parts. Yet the practice continued, and the reason it continued was cost. In new product development, some subassemblies are scrapped after testing because changes must be made. By building the model only after the part was certain to be used, development groups can save $10,000 to $20,000. Broadly applied, this wait-and-see attitude could shave $20,000 to $50,000 off the cost of product development.

This sounds fine except for one thing: Delays in development mean lost profits. Because of the increasing pace of technological innovation, new products have shorter life cycles, and each product must be brought to the market as quickly as possible. A delay in bringing a new product to the market can cost Dynapert $100,000 in lost profits per month. Thus, a three-month delay in the introduction of a new project may save the company $50,000 in product development costs—but *cost* the company *$300,000* in lost profits. In the long run, cost-avoidance was a costly strategy.

Companies lose untold millions of dollars in profits this way. And this was not a situation where Dynapert was debating the costs and risks of developing a new product. A strategic opportunity had already been identified, the market for the product had been proven, and the decision to go ahead with it had been made. Yet the product development phase was not viewed in strategic terms—what the new product can *produce* for the company—but simply in terms of cost. In this way, the Dynapert story reflects the basic strategic shortsightedness that has afflicted U.S. manufacturing and contributed to its downfall.

More than high labor costs or obsolete plant equipment, this lack of strategic vision has contributed to the downfall of American manufacturing. I believe this erosion of strategic vision manifests itself in three ways, all of which carry lessons for us as we reshape and rebuild the manufacturing sector: (1) Management strategies of the sixties and early seventies, which placed financial return above a company's ability to produce and develop its own product, unwittingly began the decline; (2) once this decline began, deeply entrenched cultures within corporations served as barriers to further progress; and (3) the weaknesses that developed invited invasion of the U.S. market by overseas competitors.

Financially Oriented Management Strategies

As the United States' prosperity increased in the sixties, management strategies were developed to reflect the manufacturing conditions of the time—and these conditions were dramatically changed from those of previous decades. As the National Academy of Engineering's recent report, *U.S. Leadership in Manufacturing,* pointed out, in the post–World War II era industrial companies were run by executives who had spent a lifetime in the business. They knew their products, and they intuitively understood the kinds of technological risks that might be necessary to stay on top of the field. But when these industrial companies were merged into conglomerates in the sixties—the so-called go-go years on Wall Street—the old-line manufacturing executives vanished.

They were replaced by financially oriented and acquisition-minded executives who had no firsthand experience with the manufacturing process. These new executives had a much different view of how to run a manufacturing operation. They had no pride of creation in any particular product. They were concerned primarily with comparisons between competing investments, and the evaluation of financial performance emphasized extremely short-term time horizons (as it still does today). When these practices first became popular in the sixties, they seemed to make sense, but beginning in the early seventies they contributed to the initial decline of U.S. manufacturing.

Capital Investments

From our vantage point in the late 1980s, living in the world of junk bonds and internationally financed debt, it is hard to remember that during the sixties capital was actually hard to come by. It was (and oddly enough, is still today) allocated as a scarce resource; to obtain capital within a company, manufacturing executives had to prove that their proposal could compete favorably with other uses of the money.

And to financially oriented corporate executives in the sixties and seventies, alternative investments often looked more profitable than actually investing funds in product development. Beginning in the sixties U.S. capital investment fell far behind that of our industrial competitors. According to a 1982 National Academy of Sciences study, between 1960 and 1978, capital investment as a percentage of output was 9.2 percent in the United States, compared with 15.9 percent in West Germany and 28.8 percent in Japan. As the technology of manufacturing advanced rapidly, industrial plants in the United States became obsolete, and the quality of U.S. products diminished rapidly.

Much has been written on this problem, but one element of it has not been adequately addressed or completely understood: the way manufacturing managers *reacted* to this reduction in investment for new capital equipment. When manufacturing managers could not get funds for new capital equipment, they frequently compensated by hiring semi-skilled workers to perform tasks that machines should have done. At first this influx of labor solved the problem of underinvestment, but as time went on labor became far more expensive. I believe that at least 25 percent of all the jobs in manufacturing were created unnecessarily as the result of capital starvation some twenty years ago.

Let me use the Singer Company, where I once worked, as an example. Twenty years ago, Singer was the world's leading manufacturer and marketer of consumer sewing machines. In 1968, however, Singer management embarked on a strategy of diversification. The sewing machine business was considered a cash cow whose profits could be used to finance mergers and acquisitions. To produce more funds for diversification, capital expenditures in the sewing segment of the company were significantly reduced.

During this period, however, Singer's sewing machine competitors—particularly the Japanese—introduced new machines with dramatically different styling and many new features. These new machines began to compete successfully with Singer in the marketplace. The Sewing Products Group's marketing organization concluded that the Singer line had to be upgraded in order to protect the company's declining market share. So the marketing people prodded the engineering departments to begin working on improved sewing machines that could compete against the onslaught of Japanese and European models.

In designing these new machines, the Singer engineers also decided to take advantage of new manufacturing technologies. They tightened the tolerances on their manufacturing tools—that is, they designed the tools so that parts could be produced directly to the required precision without any additional machining. But to hold these tolerances, Singer had to develop new manufacturing processes. These processes would eliminate a considerable amount of machine work and assembly-line labor—but they were expensive.

Thus, the capital expense needed for these new machines mounted rapidly. But because Singer's policy was to use its financial resources for acquisitions and mergers, the Sewing Products Group could not get the necessary capital funds from the company.

The resourceful people in manufacturing and engineering at Singer, however, were not stopped by the rejection of their request for capital funds. After all, they were under attack from sewing machine competitors around the world. They decided that the only way to obtain the money necessary to produce the new model was to redesign the machine so that it would use less costly capital equipment.

One way to accomplish this goal, they saw, was to open up the parts tolerances so that the existing capital equipment could be used to manufacture it. Of course, the new sewing process would still need the tighter tolerances originally specified. But this tightening of the tolerances could be achieved on the assembly line. Instead of achieving the precision through the use of costly capital equipment for more precision tools, the manufacturing managers simply added twenty or thirty seconds to the assembly line by having an operator adjust the settings manually.

The result was dramatic: the cost of capital the new machine was reduced significantly simply by shifting some requirements from capital to labor. Twenty years ago, labor was not all that costly, and the addition of a twenty-second adjustment on the assembly line was a good tradeoff for several million dollars worth of capital equipment.

As a result, Singer approved the new machine, and at first it was a success. But as the cost of assembly labor increased, the twenty-second adjustments did not look like such a good deal. A decade later, because labor costs grew, these adjustments caused a dramatic increase in the cost of the machine—which made it harder than ever to keep up with foreign competitors.

Because Singer was not willing to invest capital funds in its best-known and most successful product, unnecessary assembly-line jobs were created. In the context of the times, the strategy made sense: Capital funds could be put to more profitable use elsewhere, and a minor adjustment in labor cost could compensate for a lack of capital investment.

Yet it was a shortsighted solution. Singer could have solved the production problem forever. Instead, the company compensated for the problem with labor, yet labor was something over which the company had only limited control—as it discovered years later, when labor costs began to mount. In other words, Singer's strategy saved capital funds for other purposes, but made the product's competitiveness largely dependent on the cost of labor. As U.S. workers became more expensive compared to their foreign counterparts, the cost of the original Singer decision mounted.

Today, many U.S. manufacturing companies make the same mistake, and choose to outsource manufacturing operations to low-wage countries rather than pursue technological innovation. But who can predict that workers in Korea or Mexico, on whom those companies are now dependent for competitiveness, will be low-wage workers ten or twenty years from now?

Furthermore, a company that chooses low-wage labor over capital investment can sometimes lose the technological edge. In an article included in *Harvard Business Review*'s booklet, *Manufacturing: Reconsidering Old Solutions*, William K. Hall notes that in the early sixties, Tappan—then the market leader in kitchen ranges—chose to outsource manufacturing activities and reduce investment in new technology. It worked in the short run, but today Tappan has paid the price because the company has fallen behind its competitors in the development of low-priced microwave ovens.

The Justification Process

As I have pointed out, if U.S. companies implement advanced technological solutions quickly and willingly, they can prevent many of the problems that Singer and Tappan experienced. Yet many still do not do so. The problem is not that we don't know about these strategies or don't know how to use them. Rather, it's an updated version of the problem Singer ran into twenty years ago: Our corporate leaders rarely grant our manufacturing managers permission to use them.

The reason is the justification process—the method by which we justify the expenditure of funds in order to obtain approval from the executive suite. Outmoded methods of justification are quite likely the single biggest barrier to the use of new manufacturing technologies—particularly automated technologies—by U.S. companies.

The justification process is the heart of good capital expenditure management. We have to have some measurement of the investment worth of individual proposals. But in order to measure how good a project is, we must have the right kind of yardstick.

Traditional justification yardsticks don't measure the right things any more. They are almost always based on some internal rate of return or payback period. A *hurdle rate*—that is, a rate of return that had to be met in order to make the investment worthwhile—was established, and investments that cleared the hurdle rate got approval. If none of the proposed investments achieved the hurdle rate, then nothing was done—and that was considered the best alternative at the time.

As Jay Tracy O'Rourke, president and chief executive officer of the Allen Bradley Company, has pointed out, these return-on-investment methods date back to the days when managers could anticipate a relatively stable economy, a relatively stable market, relatively stable manufacturing technologies—and, of course, when capital was a scarce resource to be allocated. Hurdle rates were the same for all businesses. In such an environment, it was easy to see the investment alternatives.

The world has changed. One business may grow at 3 percent per year and another at 50 percent per year, yet despite the disparity in growth both may be considered healthy (or in some fast-paced industries, unhealthy). Manufacturing technologies are advancing at rates far too fast to track. Customers are still concerned with price, but quality is often more important. With worldwide competition, high-risk strategies become necessary—because if you don't make a high-risk investment, someone on some other continent will. Capital is available through new instruments to raise funds, while innovative people and ideas are scarce.

In this kind of environment, the old justification techniques no longer make sense. For example, how can traditional justification systems evaluate a world in which quality is at least as important as price—and probably more important in many segments? How do managers use the old yardstick to measure the value of a well-engineered product that sells for perhaps 2 to 3 percent more than its competitors but provides 10 percent more value? Like capital expenditure policies, the new hurdle rate must be conceived of in terms of strategic value and not financial return.

Industrial Cultures as Barriers

These management practices from the sixties and seventies clearly helped to initiate serious problems in American manufacturing. But as problems grew, deeply entrenched cultures within those companies built barriers that exacerbated problems. Chief among these in manufacturing companies—both on the shop floor and in the corporate office—were the cultures of industrial engineering, quality control, short-term return, and sales.

The Culture of Industrial Engineering

In the past, "scientific" management of factories sought to increase productivity by reducing work to a series of simple, routine tasks and by centralizing managerial control as much as possible. Because so much repetitive work had to be done by humans, the goal was to make productivity as much as possible independent of the motivation of the individual worker. Thus, the traditional American factory from Henry Ford onward was designed to minimize discretion of those on the shop floor so that high productivity could be obtained with only a limited commitment from the work force.

This philosophy was immortalized in the work of Frederick Winslow Taylor, often called the father of modern industry. Taylor believed that the work of a factory should be divided into a series of small, discrete tasks. Drawings should be prepared by draftsmen in the drawing room, polishing should be done in the polishing room by polishers, and so on. In fact, Taylor once wrote, "Under our system, a worker is told just what he is to do and how he is to do it. Any improvement he makes on the orders given him is fatal to his success."

When Alfred P. Sloan organized General Motors, he institutionalized the Taylor method by organizing the entire company into functional units such as engineering, manufacturing, and selling. These organizations were based on the notion that a corporation was grounded in manufacturing, even though finance, transportation, communications, and other departments played increasingly larger roles.

This method was well suited to its time. In those days, four out of every five employees at a company such as GM were either manufacturing or clerical workers doing routine tasks. Like other companies, GM was essentially a single-product, single-technology, single-market business. Corporate survival at GM, as elsewhere, was based on the ability to manage superbly.

Today, however, corporations are multiproduct, multi-technology, and multimarket entities. They are not necessarily conglomerates, but they usually are diversified. Fewer workers perform routine tasks; the work involves more knowledge on the part of employees. Corporate managers must be more entrepreneurial in the sense that they must be able to adapt to change rather than simply manage what lies below them on the organizational chart. These changes have rendered the Taylor method, once well suited to a manufacturing operation, obsolete.

Some of the best Japanese companies have come to understand this more quickly than we have. Konosuke Matushita issued a warning to American executives when he said not long ago,

> Your firms are built on the Taylor model. Even worse, so are your heads. With your bosses doing the thinking while workers wield the screwdrivers, you're convinced deep down that this is the right way to run a business. We are beyond the Taylor model. Business, we know, is now so complex and difficult, the survival of firms so hazardous, in an environment increasingly unpredictable, competitive, and fraught with danger that their continued existence depends on the day-to-day mobilization of every ounce of intelligence.

Conditions change more easily than managers, however.

Although traditional needs have disappeared, managers (like myself) have been trained in the Taylor tradition of industrial engineering. At the time of our education, the Taylor method was *the* model of efficiency. Today, however, it is the model of inefficiency—locking factories into outmoded methods of performing tasks and moving materials around the plant. Now that specialization and quality are more important than low product cost, our factories can no longer compete with those overseas.

The Culture of Quality Control

There are many explanations for why the Japanese have achieved a competitive position in manufacturing, but on one nearly every observer is unanimous: Their products are of high quality. As Japanese products get better, their competitiveness improves; conversely, as the United States loses its competitive position, the quality of U.S. products decreases.

I don't ordinarily like to point to the Japanese and say we should do things their way because I don't believe that techniques that arise out of Japanese culture can be applied successfully in the American workplace. But quality control is an exception. Once the Japanese learned to concentrate on making products right in the first place, U.S. manufacturing was instantly at a disadvantage. When our companies tried to fight back, they did so without abandoning the culture of quality control, which put them at a further disadvantage. As with industrial engineering, the entire manufacturing process had been arranged around the goal of *controlling* quality rather than *creating* it. Conditions had changed, but long-held assumptions hadn't been challenged.

The Culture of Short-Term Return

In the 1960s, the financially oriented executives who began to replace old-line manufacturing chiefs brought with them a new culture that was to work against them: the short-term culture.

The short-term culture values quarterly profits over long-term stability, and was quite directly generated by the financially oriented goals of the executives who rose to the top of U.S. corporations in the sixties and seventies. Moreover, those executives realize that the financial success of corporations in the United States is tightly linked to investors through a highly volatile machine that changes virtually every second—the stock market. As Edward L. Hennessy, chairman and CEO of Allied Signal, Incorporated, has pointed out, U.S. companies use debt financing for only about 30 percent of their capital, while Japanese and German companies "go to the bank" about 65 percent of the time. That means U.S. firms are much more tied to the volatility and short-term expectations of stock-market investors than their Western industrial competitors. Investors want to maximize return, so they examine daily stock returns and quarterly and annual reports. Bankers and financial analysts who serve these investors want to show results, so they too look at short-term profits. And the business press—which feeds off and perpetuates the attitude of Wall Street insiders—focuses on short-term profits as well.

The short-term culture really came into its own during the economic ups and downs of the seventies. Uncertain about when the next recession might hit, executives and investors both became more volatile, flitting from company to company in hopes of getting the best immediate return as a hedge against the future. In particular, as a National Academy of Engineering symposium on manufacturing recently pointed out, the high cost of money forced U.S. industrial companies to compress their time horizons. Many companies sought short-term market payoffs or diversified through acquisitions and shortchanged research and development and capital investment.

For manufacturing, however, the natural pace of innovation is far different from the Wall Street–driven pace of the short-term culture. It can take three years, five years, or even more to carry out a strategic plan or to develop and then commercialize an innovation. Yet top executives in U.S. industrial corporations rarely think beyond the current quarter or the current year.

This short-term attitude became painfully clear to industrial managers and executives shortly after the so-called stock crash in October 1987. Because of the long period of economic growth during the eighties, many companies had the luxury of planning strategically about the future—and, in particular, planning for the use of new technologies to combat overseas competitors. In one day, the stock plunge changed all that. Top corporate executives immediately put most of their plans on hold or scrapped them and scrambled for quick fixes that would continue to make their companies look good to Wall Street investors. When executives perceived that a downturn in the U.S. economy was coming, they stopped trying to position themselves for the future.

These executives made a mistake—not in halting plans for future innovation, because recessions inevitably occur and aggressive innovation inevitably is curtailed while everyone waits for the recovery, but in forgetting their strategic vision. Even during an economic crisis, they ought to hang on to it.

The Culture of Sales

In the mid-1960s I went to work at a bustling industrial plant at 1200 Babbitt Road in the Cleveland suburb of Euclid, Ohio—the home of what was then known as Addressograph/Multigraph or AM. At this plant I witnessed firsthand how a sales-oriented culture can ultimately lead to the demise of a product and even a company.

The company was a market leader in its time. Everyone carried Addressograph's metal department store charge plates. And everyone sent memos duplicated on Addressograph/Multigraph offset duplicators and mailed out on Addressograph label printers.

AM's engineering and manufacturing divisions were concerned primarily with developing and producing extensions of their existing product lines. Any effort to explore new technologies was discouraged on the theory that the company's job was to "keep the factories humming." Eventually, of course, those new technologies—particularly computer-generated mailing labels and photocopy reproduction technology—drove AM into bankruptcy.

In the end, AM was too enamored of its own market leadership, its products, its technology—and especially its expensive capital facilities, which the company wrongly believed would shield it from competition. Even as computers produced monthly reports and photocopiers churned away throughout AM's factories, management could not see the threat of new technology. And the company's complacency was further encouraged by financial analysts who reacted favorably to the company's short-term success and helped drive up stock prices.

Though it's now several years old, the AM story remains a striking example of how a sales-oriented culture can undermine an otherwise healthy manufacturing company. Another example is the auto industry in the seventies, which believed that it could continue to persuade American consumers to buy large cars loaded with options because they were more profitable for the companies.

This thinking pervaded many U.S. companies in the sixties and seventies. These companies convinced themselves that they did not need to push for innovation but could simply continue pushing what they had always sold. The narrowmindedness of the sales culture and the cultures of quality control and industrial engineering—combined with the short-term return culture of the financially oriented management then emerging—opened the door for a foreign invasion.

The Invasion of Global Competitors

The invasion of the U.S. market by foreign manufacturers, then, was not due entirely to low-cost labor. Japan and countries in Europe, with comparable wage scales, cleverly pounced on several U.S. manufacturing and marketing weaknesses.

We didn't take foreign competition seriously—at least not at first. Take, for example, RCA, which had a long lead in the color television market but was unable to capitalize on that lead to quash the Japanese invasion.

RCA was once the indisputable leader in the development of color television. After achieving its lead, however, RCA decided to move into the electronic data processing field. Color TV was the cash cow that made this move possible. In order to funnel the funds into computers, RCA cut back on color television research and development, kept the prices of sets high, and licensed patents freely—especially to the Japanese. As a result, RCA's share of the color TV market declined steadily. What could have been RCA's domain for decades became a battlefield for the more aggressive and eventually more successful Japanese firms.

One of the major industrial blunders of the postwar period was the failure of U.S. consumer electronics companies such as RCA to move into the Japanese market at a time when they might have controlled it. Many firms in other industries, from textiles to steels, ignored the Japanese market. But few provided the Japanese with more unwitting assistance than RCA.

The Japanese move began in 1949, when Sony purchased a license to manufacture transistors from Bell Labs for $25,000. At AT&T there was no interest in consumer electronics; other U.S. companies believed transistors would never replace tubes in consumer items. I worked at RCA during this period and recall the company's attempts to develop a miniaturized electronic vacuum tube as a means of combatting the transistor. But even as the Japanese firms increased their share of the U.S. radio market from 2 percent in 1955 to 93 percent in 1973, U.S. companies did not feel threatened. Radio was an outmoded technology. RCA, Zenith, and other companies were concentrating on television.

The radio experience should have alerted the Americans to the challenge of the Japanese. But for many reasons, this did not happen. For one thing, after fifteen years of intense and costly competition, the television industry in the United States had stabilized in the late sixties. The market was still expanding, and there seemed to be room for all.

Furthermore, there was little reason to believe in the sixties that the Japanese might invade the U.S. television market in a meaningful way. In 1962 Japanese TVs were being sold for a third less than the same size RCA models, but they weren't well received—the assumption at the time being that the label ''Made in Japan'' connoted inferior workmanship.

The monumental indifference to the Japanese threat was evidenced in 1963, when RCA cut off negotiations to manufacture color televisions for Sears, Roebuck that would be sold under the Sears name. RCA founder David Sarnoff felt his position was so dominant that he could dictate such terms. Zenith and other U.S. manufacturers took the same stance against Sears.

This made sense in the short run. In 1963 public demand for color TV outpaced production capacity, and color sets were the single most vigorous growth component of the consumer electronics market. There also was considerable fear that if RCA, which dominated the consumer electronics industry, made a deal with Sears, which dominated the retail market, the U.S. Justice Department's antitrust lawyers might cause problems. (In fact, part of RCA's fear was that Sears's sales organization was so strong that it could outmuscle RCA in the long run.)

At the same time, however, the major Japanese manufacturers—Hitachi, Matsushita (Panasonic), Sony, and Toshiba—came together with the Japanese government's blessing to form the Television Export Council and the Television

Export Examination Committee and devise a strategy for cracking the U.S. market. Their idea was to sell TV sets as cheaply as possible, gain market share, force out American competitors, and then raise prices in order to realize profits.

So when RCA turned down Sears, Sony was more than happy to produce as many sets as Sears wanted, to Sears's specifications, for a lower price than RCA demanded. Between 1963 and 1977 Sears purchased 6.5 million Japanese sets from Sony and later Toshiba.

Unwittingly, RCA assisted the Japanese—indeed, RCA made Japanese color television possible by selling them all the technology licenses they asked for. The Japanese, of course, were entirely dependent on foreign sources for technology. This was a highly profitable exercise for RCA, which, at one point, was earning almost as much money from the licenses as from the sale of the actual products. Nor was RCA alone. Of all the U.S.-Japanese licensing agreements in place in 1970, three-quarters were for videotape players, semiconductors, tubes, and other components used in consumer electronics. Little wonder that as late as 1965, the Japanese spent only six cents on research and development for every dollar the Americans spent.

The result: Between 1963 and 1974, electronic imports rose from 7 percent of the American market to 40 percent— and the new world leader in the field was not RCA but Matsushita, the parent company to Panasonic. Though they had made considerable strides in color television (20 percent by the early seventies or about the same as RCA), the Japanese had used the Americans' obsession with color TV to invade the market by concentrating on other supposedly outdated products. By 1974 their domination of these other electronic markets was so total that not a single American corporation even manufactured radios, tape recorders, or black-and-white TVs.

In fact, by the late seventies the Japanese were controlling not only electronics markets but electronics technology as well. When RCA emerged as the leading marketer of videocassette recorders in the United States, it was using Japanese technology. By using a licensing agreement with Matsushita, RCA was able to beat off a challenge by Zenith—which had become a licensee of Sony. In less than a generation, the roles had been completely reversed.

The RCA case is not an isolated one. Companies in many other sectors in the economy made the same mistakes. Xerox, for example, surrendered the low-cost copier market to the Japanese on the assumption that it would never be a large enough market to be worth pursuing. However, once low-cost Japanese copiers were introduced in the United States, they created their own market—many more copies were being made as a result—and Xerox had to catch up to the Japanese. Over and over again, U.S. companies were slow to recognize the strategic opportunities manufacturing offered, and as a result, over and over again, the Japanese gained a competitive advantage.

Lessons for the Future

In criticizing American corporate strategies I don't mean to suggest that they were wrong at the time. Justification and compensation methods based purely on financial return seemed to make sense at a time when markets were stable and capital was scarce. Job classifications that emphasized division of labor into discrete parts were a natural outgrowth of a time when manufacturing assembly processes inevitably involved large amounts of human labor. A corporate leader like David Sarnoff had every reason to believe that the U.S. Justice Department was a bigger threat to his color-television empire than the Japanese.

My purpose in outlining these reasons behind the decline of U.S. manufacturing is to show that all is not lost. The conditions that prevailed at the same time *do not* exist today. Capital is not scarce. Product assembly no longer requires large amounts of human capital. The federal government now is more concerned with economic competition between the United States and other nations than economic competition between RCA and Sears. Indeed, manufacturing itself is no longer simply the game of producing huge amounts of low-cost product as cheaply as possible.

One condition has *not* changed, however: To be successful, manufacturing must be important within the corporate realm. The corporate leaders mentioned in this chapter made the mistake of ignoring manufacturing or taking it for granted. Today's corporate leaders cannot afford to continue to do so. They must understand that they need manufacturing to survive—and that the opportunities are at hand to use it strategically.

Even if manufacturing is regarded as important in the corporate suite, however, the opportunities it presents must be fully developed. Sometimes merely mechanizing is not enough; one must also rethink the process. This means that companies must change and understand the nature of change. In the following chapters, I discuss these agents of change and describe the opportunities they present.

Part II

Rethinking Manufacturing

3

The Factory of Opportunity

Mallory Timers Company is the leading supplier of timers to the appliance business. Whirlpool, Maytag, General Electric, White, and many other appliance leaders are among Mallory's customers. But staying competitive is not easy. Mallory must supply its customers with more than 200 types of timers. The number of new model variations is literally infinite. And increasingly, Mallory's customers don't want to warehouse the inventory; they want Mallory to deliver the exact number of timers they need at the moment those timers are needed. That means Mallory must warehouse the timers itself, which is expensive, or else learn to produce varying lots quickly and efficiently. The company has chosen the latter course.

The obvious solution—the one most in keeping with conventional wisdom in manufacturing—was automation: the replacement of assembly-line workers with robots and computers. In fact, Mallory's solution did involve automation. Mallory is owned by my company, Emhart, which was able to provide it with financial support for a programmable automation system. This system combines ten robots with other elements of automation to create a high-speed, flexible assembly line.

To Automate: Bring Engineering and Manufacturing Together

But automation at Mallory involved more than robots and a computer-integrated manufacturing (CIM) system. As it instituted a programmable automation system Mallory also worked to redesign its timers to make them easier for the new system to assemble. This required designers and manufacturing engineers—people who traditionally have little to do with each other—to work closely together to make the product cheaper and easier to assemble. Rather than simply "mechanizing the process," they ultimately reduced the required number of parts and in many instances created a different kind of part—parts that were "designed for assembly." These parts are designed so they flow freely along the conveyor system without tangling or otherwise slowing down the process.

A more efficient production system would have been reward enough, but Mallory found its new system resulted in another bonus—better quality. To keep the automated assembly process moving, the quality of the pieces must be kept high. In addition, automatic inspection devices segregate rejected or incomplete products at each stage of the manufacturing process, rather than at the end. This means fewer defects and—for Mallory—lower warranty costs.

Thus, in seeking to become more competitive through automation, Mallory succeeded because it did not stop simply at automation. It brought design and manufacturing closer together in redesigning the products—a working relationship that will pay off again and again in product development. And it also improved the quality of its products. In seeking to create what most manufacturing executives would call the factory of the future, Mallory had made full use of what I call the factory of opportunity. The $6 million investment is expected to recoup the company $2 million a year just in lower warranty costs.

Opportunity, as it is typically defined these days by American corporate leaders with reference to manufacturing, generally means automation and nothing more. In rhapsodizing about the factory of the future, they envision lights-out plants where mechanized devices work all night making products with minimal assistance from expensive human laborers.

There's no question that to prosper, manufacturing plants must have fewer assembly-line jobs. But we cannot solve manufacturing woes simply by replacing workers with robots. Even if we replaced every worker in the United States with a robot, our manufacturing processes would still produce excess inventory, excess scrap, or poor-quality products. Our manufacturing would not be improved because our approach to manufacturing would not have changed.

As the Mallory example shows, instead of focusing only on technological improvements such as robotics, we must go a step further and recognize that the nature of manufacturing has changed. When the U.S. corporate structure took shape in the fifties and sixties, the United States' economy was largely independent from the rest of the world. Markets were stable and growing, and success came to the company that could produce the lowest-cost product in the least amount of time with the lowest labor cost. The cost of entering the market for most manufactured products was so high it virtually shut out new competitors.

But that world has vanished. Today U.S. manufacturing companies are engaged in a fast-paced global competition for markets, labor, suppliers, and raw materials. That competition accelerates every day, fueled by remarkably rapid advances in technology. Products and manufacturing processes are much more complex, requiring wide-ranging and extremely expensive research skills and facilities. Markets are volatile and unpredictable, affected not just by demand but by currency fluctuations, trade policies, and determined foreign rivals subsidized by their home governments.

As a result, the goals of manufacturing today are completely different than they were fifteen or twenty years ago: Instead of striving to simply produce low-cost products, manufacturers need to create innovative products that meet new market needs, develop them over a shorter time period, and respond to a market that is more demanding in terms of quality, reliability, and flexibility. With so many factors hurtling headlong at U.S. manufacturers, it's extremely difficult for corporate executives and plant managers to maintain control over their companies' competitive position.

Yet the forces that have changed manufacturing so dramatically also opened new areas of opportunity that American companies can take advantage of. That is why I call the factory of the future the factory of opportunity.

Needed—An Overall, Integrated Vision of Manufacturing

The factory of opportunity is completely different from the factory of the past—not just in its machinery but also in its orientation. Scrap must be used, not thrown away. Products must be made right in the first place, rather than made wrong and then weeded out through inspection. Faster turnaround times and greater flexibility must be accommodated, even though traditional thinking would dictate the low-cost manufacture of identical products on identical schedules. High added-value products—that is, products where a great deal of value is added in the manufacturing process—must be targeted as appropriate products for U.S. factories. Most of all, *manufacturing, design, marketing, and other functions must be integrated* to achieve a new kind of efficiency in factories— an efficiency that will permit this new flexibility and still keep U.S. prices competitive.

It is true that fewer semi-skilled factory workers will be needed in the factory of opportunity. But many jobs will— or should—become less repetitive, and more technicians, maintenance personnel, and experts in materials and information will be needed. If technological advances can help reduce errors and improve quality, they also must be used to make the factory less dreary and to help attract bright and able young people into knowledge-intensive, skill-oriented jobs.

Though the magnitude of these changes can be disorienting, many of them are ideally suited to U.S. companies and the American work force. Innovation, flexibility, shorter time periods—all these are areas in which U.S. factories can be just as responsive and competitive as factories anywhere else in the world. And these are the reasons that U.S. factories can become strategic weapons for U.S. corporations seeking to survive in the global economy.

Consider the recent well-publicized success stories about companies such as IBM and Xerox, which remain market leaders despite high prices. We sometimes forget that the Japanese first cracked the U.S. market with inexpensive products in many fields, but as their expenses have mounted, Japanese companies have retained or strengthened their lead by building a reputation for quality, reliability, innovation, and flexibility.

Fuji, for example, has begun to challenge Kodak, which once had a virtual monopoly on photographic supplies, not because its products are cheaper or better but because Fuji has been able to bring the latest advances onto the market quickly. Fuji has used its ability to convert technology advances into manufactured products rapidly as a strategic weapon and did not achieved success because of low wages or any other inherently non-American trait. In fact, Kodak's management could have achieved the same results—and may have to, now that Fuji is pushing Kodak hard.

Too often, U.S. companies try to remain competitive by using the same techniques they used twenty-five years ago. They bring new machines into the factory, but they don't examine how to use the machine's full potential to improve the factory's efficiency. They make strategic corporate decisions based on financial analyses that assume stable and growing markets. They lay off factory workers but don't take steps to make the remaining employees more productive.

For example, the so-called panaceas that have been foisted on our factories in the last few years—quality circles, just-in-time inventory policies, robotics—all recognize that the nature of manufacturing has changed. But U.S. manufacturing companies that use them have failed to recognize that these changes must be dealt with at their most basic and comprehensive level. They don't view the entire manufacturing process as a whole and deal with it that way. Instead, they seek to attribute this country's manufacturing ills to one oversimplified problem—labor costs, low productivity, excess inventory—and believe that the entire manufacturing sector can be rejuvenated by dealing with that problem. In short, too many U.S. manufacturing companies have ignored the need to take a broad, integrated view of the factory. As the Manufacturing Studies Board's recent report on manufacturing firms in the United States pointed out, "Manufacturing is not limited to the material transformations performed in a factory. It is a *system* encompassing design, engineering, purchasing, quality control, marketing, and customer service as well as material transformation; the operations of the subcontractors and the whims of customers are also important parts of the system." In other words, U.S. manufacturing companies must change constantly. They must *rethink* their businesses—over and over again—to remain competitive.

Change frightens many people. Even the open-minded factory manager may find the idea of rethinking the business's approach overwhelming. Yet embracing and using change is the only hope manufacturers have to remain strong because it represents their only opportunity to retain some control over their own businesses.

In the next five chapters I examine in detail five areas of change that must be mastered if U.S. manufacturers are to remain strong. Two—technological advances and global forces—are agents of change, pushing U.S. corporations into a new environment whether they want to go or not. The other three—finance, human resources, and external relationships—are areas that are inevitably affected by change and must respond effectively if U.S. manufacturing is to prosper. Though each is potentially overwhelming, each also represents an opportunity. All five must work together. A technological solution such as robotics is of little use unless factory managers also understand its effect on people and on the global market, for example. Management policies in one area will, in effect, become management policies in all five.

Because of traditional thinking, panic, and the panacea syndrome, these five areas of change—and the relationships among them—have not been well understood by U.S. manufacturers. Technological panaceas, for example, have not taken into account how they affect a company's human resources or how technology can be made more effective through external relationships. U.S. factories have attempted to confront global forces alone, without the help of available outside institutions and sometimes without attuning their personnel to cultural differences abroad. And so on.

However, in order to rethink our manufacturing products and processes to restore American competitiveness, we must understand and use all five together. At a time when competition and change is strong and rapid, manufacturers simply cannot waste a single opportunity to improve their competitive position. Each of these five areas present opportunities. But *together*, the five areas create—or at least illuminate—hundreds of new opportunities within the U.S. factory that can be used to remain competitive. To approach this challenge properly requires change—not just a change in technology or human resources or global strategy, but a change in the vision that springs from an understanding of how manufacturing has changed, and the power these five forces have to shape the factory of the future.

The next five chapters treats each of these five elements separately, but each is explained in the context of the other four—because attempts to capitalize on these opportunities cannot succeed any other way. Accomplished properly, this sort of change creates exciting opportunities—opportunities to give employees at all levels new and interesting jobs, to meet new market needs all over the world, and to restore manufacturing to its strategic position within the corporate structure.

4

Technology

Several years ago, Emhart's United Shoe Machinery plant in Beverly, Massachusetts faced an inventory problem. The USM plant manufactured metal stands that support shoe machinery products sold worldwide. The raw material—lengths of angle iron—didn't take up much space in the warehouse. But once the angle irons were cut and welded into the shape of a table, storage space became critical. A few hundred tables could take up a warehouse, even though that warehouse was occupied mostly by air.

The warehousing problem was a particularly costly one because the stands are a low value-added product and the cost of storing the manufactured product was many times the cost of storing the raw material. Yet little value (in sales price) was added in converting angle irons into metal stands. Thus, the cost of storing the stands sometimes exceeded the profitability of manufacturing them.

To cut down on storage space, USM manufacturing engineers at the company decided on a high-tech solution—a robot welder. Using the robot rather than human workers, the stands could be produced quickly and inexpensively whenever an order came in. The method for welding each table could be stored and called up whenever necessary, so that single stands or small lots could be manufactured. Warehousing space would not be required.

After an initial debugging period, the robot welder was a huge success. Not only could it produce stands on demand, but it could weld them faster than the workers who had done the job before the robot was purchased. It quickly became the showpiece of the entire factory.

One time when I visited the Beverly plant, however, the robot welder wasn't working. Spare parts had to be ordered from Sweden, so the robot was standing idle and human workers were welding the stands. A remarkable thing happened: People could weld just as fast as the robot—much faster than they had ever been able to weld before the robot was brought to the factory.

We could not understand why this was so until we saw that the USM manufacturing engineers had not simply used the robot to mechanize the welding process. To accommodate the robot, they had completely redesigned the product and the manufacturing process.

The human welders could adapt to sharp turns and obstacles and compensate for wide tolerances at the seams. But because the robot had only limited mobility, it required straight, tightly fitted seams with as few obstacles as possible in the welding path. So the manufacturing engineers designed a better production method, which positioned the angle iron more precisely and improved cutting to produce seams that fit together more tightly. These changes not only accommodated the robot but also made the human welders faster and more efficient.

Once the robot was repaired, it was put back into service because it still had other advantages over the human workers, particularly the ability to work for long periods of time without fatigue. But the manufacturing engineers in Beverly had learned something useful. The robot was faster and more efficient not because of its technology but because the job was designed more efficiently.

If I had to sum up the lesson of the Beverly robot welder

in one sentence, I would put it like this: *Don't just automate your manufacturing process; redesign it to accommodate automation.* Most manufacturing companies, locked into the simplistic philosophy of cost avoidance, simply purchase a new robot to replace workers on the line without thinking about the system changes that might be required in order to accommodate the new machines. The result: Inefficiencies in the manufacturing process are not eliminated but simply mechanized, thereby compounding the problem.

The thinking at the Beverly plant was not initially revolutionary: USM purchased a robot welder hoping to cut down on warehousing costs. And it's true that the robot's flashy advantages—the speed and the ability to operate without rest—made it the showpiece of the factory and the envy of other plants. But the robot's *limitations* gave the Beverly plant its competitive advantage. The human welders always could have worked faster, but until the robot was introduced, there was no reason to adjust the process or the product; the worker could do the adjusting. When faced with a mechanical welder, the manufacturing engineers were forced to examine underlying inefficiencies in the manufacture of the product.

The Beverly engineers had placed their technological advance in proper perspective. They didn't approach the robot welder as a panacea—a magic machine that would solve all their problems—but rather as a useful tool that would help make their plant more efficient and competitive.

Simply speeding up the assembly process—with all its inefficiencies and mistakes—is not good enough. As earlier chapters have indicated, manufacturing no longer can simply make standard units as quickly and cheaply as possible. Today it is in the business of satisfying the needs of customers who are interested in quality, reliability, and customization. Technological advances must be used to assist manufacturing executives in *rethinking* their operations in order to meet those needs.

The Typical Approach: Leap before You Look

Technology is often the first love of manufacturing plant managers. They are drawn to factories and remain there because of their ability to work with machines. Remarkably enough, these plant managers sometimes suffer from myopia when they look at the possibilities of advanced technology systems, and this myopia harms the competitiveness of U.S. factories every bit as much as the high cost of labor.

Consider the flexible manufacturing system, one of the most powerful tools for automation in the modern factory. Though it is not necessarily automated, a flexible manufacturing system is designed to permit factories to switch over quickly from one product to another. It is specifically designed to help plant managers take full advantage of new opportunities in the factory and respond quickly to demanding customers' needs.

Yet what happens in practice? In many U.S. factories, the answer is all too predictable.

In 1984 Harvard Business School professor Ramchandran Jaikumar compared the use of flexible manufacturing systems by manufacturing companies in Japan and the United States. He found that the average U.S. company used the system to produce ten different types of parts—but the average Japanese company, using flexible manufacturing to greater advantage, produced ninety-three. On the average, the Japanese produced twenty-two new types of parts on their flexible manufacturing systems for every one new type of part produced by their American counterparts. As Jaikumar put it, "With few exceptions, the flexible manufacturing systems installed in the United States showed an outstanding lack of flexibility."

These results have nothing to do with the technological capability of the systems; that capability was comparable. Rather, the Japanese were more willing to shed the traditional manufacturing model (high volume, low cost, identical product) when the market demanded it and technological tools allowed it. The Americans, on the other hand, were not applying their technology. They simply were acquiring it and going about their business the same old way.

This example shows how easy it is to confuse flexibility with flexible manufacturing systems. To change a machine or process rapidly in order to accommodate a different product may or may not require flexible manufacturing equipment. But it most certainly requires flexibility on the part of the factory and its workers.

Like *flexibility, integration* is an important word in discussions about modern manufacturing equipment. Many plant managers purchase a single piece of automated equipment to solve a particular problem—slow manufacture of parts, for example—with no thought to an overall strategy or to the eventual link of automated machines into some sort of computer-integrated system. A factory may purchase a new piece of machinery that can produce parts more quickly— and then batch those parts or simply stack them on the factory floor until they are used in assembly. Sometimes a million or more parts are stacked up, making it practically impossible for shop-floor workers to get to their stations.

In a traditional factory, this made sense. Parts were slow to manufacture. They required paperwork to catalogue. And it was impossible to time things perfectly so that a constant flow of necessary parts was ensured.

In the modern factory, however, this lack of overall strategy is totally unnecessary. With computerized tracking systems, plant managers can track every part and ensure that those parts arrive in the right place at the right time. Furthermore, computerized plant scheduling systems avoid the need to produce parts in advance and stack them up. Their manufacture can be postponed until they are needed elsewhere, and at that time the ability to produce parts more rapidly becomes a true advantage.

For example, Xerox's factory in Fremont, California, produces 1,000 Xerox/Diablo daisy-wheel printers and Memorywriter electronic typewriters every day. But parts aren't batched. They're marked with bar-code labels, allowing a central computer to track all parts at all times. The computer controls over 800 feet of conveyor highways and 14,000 storage locations to keep the assembly operation moving smoothly—without a million parts stacked up on the factory floor.

Taking the Quantum Leap

As the Xerox example shows, if old-fashioned manufacturing management thinking can be overcome, the payoff can be great. If a company and its managers can use technological advances to think broadly about the nature of their business, they can take a quantum leap beyond the competition. So-called technological panaceas can be made more effective, and competitiveness can be restored.

To understand how best to incorporate technological advances, I believe a company must take three steps: (1) Manufacturing managers must *think through the problem,* so that the nature of their manufacturing needs—as opposed to the nature of the new machine—are truly understood; (2) designers must learn to *design for automation*—that is, design manufactured products so they can be assembled easily and efficiently by automated machines; and (3) corporate executives must learn to take full advantage of the *competitive edge* provided by breakthroughs in automation, so that the manufacturing process is linked to sales, marketing, and other departments directly and efficiently.

Thinking Through the Problem

Step one is understanding not the machine but the reason for making or buying it. Simply automating the manufacturing process probably is going to accelerate the pace at which mistakes and inefficiencies occur. Before you decide whether to make or buy a machine using new technology, you must first make sure you *truly* understand the problem that you are trying to solve.

Let me take another example from Emhart, the company I work for. This time I would like to look at how Emhart's glass-bottle machinery group, a leader in its field, dealt with the question of automation in the glass-bottle manufacturing business.

At first glance, a factory that manufactures glass bottles may look like a model of automation because it relies heavily on pick-and-place-type robots and conveyor belts to make the assembly line operate smoothly. But the making of glass bottles remains an art because it is difficult to obtain consistency in the final product. The heart of the operation has always been skilled artisans who rely on decades of experience to make sure that the look and feel of the bottles is clean and consistent. No systematic process is involved, and costly interruptions of production lines are often required. For companies seeking to make technological advances in this field, this process represents both frustration and challenge.

Typical of the idiosyncratic processes in a glass-bottle plant is a technique called "swabbing the molds." As the glass bottles leave the molds after being formed, the machine operator often reaches into the hot molds with a stick wrapped in a wet cloth and swabs the molds with this device.

Glass-factory managers often suggested that a robot, rather than a machine operator, could be used to ensure that the swabbing took place uniformly and consistently. But the question was whether automation would achieve the same function as swabbing the molds—or merely mechanize the process without trying to understand the underlying purpose of the swabbing.

To answer this question, Bob Douglas, vice president for R&D for the Emhart glass-bottle machinery group, investigated why the molds were swabbed in the first place. As might be expected in a business that is as much art as science, he found as many answers as there were machine operators: Some said that swabbing cleaned the mold; others said it lubricated the mold. Ultimately, though, one answer began to emerge: A key factor in manufacturing consistent, high-quality bottles is the proper cooling and uniformity of the molds. Swabbing helped cool the molds uniformly.

This discovery led to the development of Emhart's axial mold-cooling system. This system does away with swabbing the molds altogether and instead uses a more efficient and effective method of reaching the same goal—jets of air channeled in and around the mold to ensure a more uniform cooling.

This breakthrough has led to increased efficiencies in the process and higher output for the industry and has allowed Emhart to take the lead in glass-container machinery, overpowering its nearest competitor, Owens-Illinois. Furthermore, because customers believe the company takes time to truly understand their processes, Emhart has gained a reputation as the most innovative company in the field. But if Emhart had not tried to think through the problem first, the company probably would have created a mechanical mold-swabber—a device that would have magnified inefficiencies in the traditional system, creating little competitive advantage for either Emhart or its customers.

It is not always easy to think through an automation problem in this way, particularly for engineers who are taught to follow rules rather than think analytically and abstractly. But any factory manager or engineer could begin an analysis of automation by taking the following steps:

1. Begin by asking why things are done the way they are. Don't assume that the way something is done now is the best way to continue doing it.
2. Examine the answers you receive for clues about the real problem. You'll get dozens of different answers, just as Emhart did on the mold-swabbing problem, but don't view them as possible solutions to the problem at hand. They are

pieces of the jigsaw puzzle you must solve in order to find out how the underlying manufacturing process works.

3. Anticipate that you will find multivariant situations. Engineers are often trained to look for one thing that's wrong and fix that single thing. In complex manufacturing systems, a series of interrelated pieces may need to be fixed or changed in some way for automation to be effective.

Designing for Automation

Step two in using technology intelligently is designing products and manufacturing processes to accommodate automation easily. The robot welder example used at the beginning of this chapter is a modest example of this sort of thinking; USM changed its manufacturing process in order to accommodate an automated machine and, in the process, made the process faster and more efficient.

But to take maximum advantage of automation, manufacturers need to take one more step and actually *design their products with automated assembly in mind.* This is an almost revolutionary idea inside a factory because it requires design and manufacturing people to maintain close contact with each other. But it can make an enormous difference in the cost of assembly.

Perhaps no company in the United States has been more successful than IBM at designing for automation to ward off foreign competition. One of IBM's biggest success stories is the Proprinter, designed for use with IBM's highly successful personal computer.

When the IBM PC was first introduced, the company turned to Epson, a leading Japanese company, to provide its printers. But in the long run, Big Blue didn't want to rely on an outside supplier, particularly a foreign company, to ensure the success of its PC and printer package, so the company decided to develop its own printer. It decided to rely heavily on robots to assemble the proprinter, but, as

IBM itself later reported, ''Installing robotics technology was not a solution in itself. Robots alone do not guarantee a more efficient and less expensive process or a better product.''

Rather, IBM began with a vision of the final product—a printer that had only 60 parts instead of 150, that operated at a speed of 200 characters per second instead of 80, and that would be easy for a robot to assemble. This last requirement forced product designers to work together with manufacturing managers at the outset of product development. As the manufacturing people outlined the limitations of robotics, the design requirements for the Proprinter were determined—no springs, no screws, no belts, and no pulleys. This translated into integrated packaging and solid connectors.

IBM's determination to use technology intelligently in developing the Proprinter forced strong, early communication between design and manufacturing and, in fact, made design the first crucial step in the manufacturing process rather than a separate process. Today, the Proprinter is assembled in a plant that links together 50 robots and 160 computers with 200 workers. Because of robotic flexibility, it is not difficult to put together the Proprinter. In IBM's words, assembling it is like ''building with children's plastic building blocks.'' Thus, it is possible to assemble Proprinters relatively inexpensively in the United States.

Though the Proprinter is probably IBM's best-known technological triumph, it is far from the only one. More impressive in many ways is the company's $350 million renovation of its Lexington, Kentucky, typewriter plant.

The Proprinter plant was started from scratch, but the Lexington plant had thirty years of history to deal with. It had long been a profitable manufacturer of Selectric typewriters, but in the early eighties the product line was aging badly. Between 1980 and 1985 the company's eight-to-one market lead in typewriters evaporated, and the number of vendors in direct competition rose from four to thirty.

The company could have chosen to move assembly to

Asia, where lower-cost labor was available, but it chose renovation in Lexington for one reason—proximity to markets. "Our markets are in the U.S. and Europe, so we didn't feel the labor savings were sufficient to offset the cost of shipping the things back," said one IBM engineer who helped to develop the manufacturing operation in the United States.

Like the Proprinter strategy, renovation of the Lexington plant was built around the idea of designing for automation. IBM wanted to be able to manufacture as many different products as possible on the same Lexington assembly line. So the company identified the characteristics and parts that were similar in different products and began building them in modules.

Previously, each machine had thousands of individual parts, but all products manufactured in Lexington (except the Selectric III, which is still assembled manually) now are made from some combination of only eleven different modules. A printer with a keyboard module added to the front becomes a typewriter; with an operational pack added to the rear, it becomes a typewriter with memory.

When IBM moved from aluminum to plastic covers, it even reduced the number of available colors for its products—from thirty-six to one. This move reflects strong, early communication between departments—in this case, between design engineers and marketing people. The marketing department at first resisted, claiming color did make a difference, but its research then revealed that customers didn't care about color. All the colors are now pearl grey—greatly reducing costs without giving up any competitive advantage.

But IBM's experience is unusual. Just as most plant managers don't rethink the manufacturing process when they acquire new technology, they don't consider whether they can make their operation more efficient (and less costly) by redesigning their products. Yet thinking through the problem is fairly simple.

In a special, September 1988 report on technology, *Man-*

ufacturing Engineering offered a few tips that designers and plant managers should keep in mind when they design for automation:

1. Reduce the number of parts needing assembly.
2. Maximize the number of parts common to different products.
3. Assemble in layers, so the parts need not be lifted or turned.
4. Add nonfunctional features—orientation parts, guide pins, chamfers—if they make the robot's job easier.
5. Design parts with similar shapes, allowing manufacturers to simplify the robot's gripper.

I would add a sixth tip to this list: Examine your parts to see how many create difficulties in assembly. Guidelines created by Geoffrey Boothroyd and Paul Dewhurst, professors at the University of Rhode Island, can help engineers measure and numerically rate the amount of difficulty any particular part will add to an automated assembly process (see "Design for Assembly: A Designer's Handbook," Warefield, R.I.: Boothroyd, Dewhurst Inc., 1983). Boothroyd's and Dewhurst's guidelines can assist in identifying parts that should be modified as well as entire products that should be reengineered because they have many parts difficult for robots to assemble.

Designing for automation is one of the most overlooked areas for potential savings in factories. Not only would most products benefit from fewer parts and more modular assembly, but designing for automation creates a close working relationship between the plant floor and the design department—a relationship that will continue to pay off as plant and design feel free to work together to make the manufacturing process more efficient.

I consider the area of designing for automation to be critical to every manufacturing strategy. (See the Appendix for a summary of various approaches to this key area.)

Using New Technology to Improve Competitiveness

The final point to be made about technology is that, properly used, it can foster competitiveness within the company. To achieve this goal, however, companies must look beyond the factory floor and see how technology can link the manufacturing process with the rest of the company's operations.

For example, Kwikset Corporation, an Emhart subsidiary that manufactures keys and locks, has just introduced its Kwiksale laptop computer ordering system, which permits a salesperson to place an order directly into the factory's production computer from the customer's office. The effect of such a system on sales and manufacturing is dramatic. It provides the sales force with a constant link to the factory, permitting sales reps to check the status of their orders and receive current information on cost and deliveries. At the factory, the need to reenter orders into the computer is eliminated, avoiding the possibility of introducing errors.

It's important to note that this technological breakthrough is not designed to eliminate the sales force. It's designed to make sales reps more effective by providing customers with a faster and more convenient way of placing their orders and making sure they are filled. An added bonus is that the system helps Kwikset cut inventory costs even further.

New technology does not automatically create competitive advantages for the plants that use it. That technology must be managed effectively by plant managers and corporate executives who use the acquisition of new technology as an opportunity to *rethink* the manufacturing process and find better ways to keep ahead of the competition. These managers and executives must identify the true nature of the problem they are working on and not merely accelerate old manufacturing processes but ferret out inefficiencies inherent in that process, using new technology to correct those inefficiencies.

Under such circumstances, the actual capability of the technology is not as important as the way it is used in the factory. It's easy to get caught up contemplating the exciting things a new machine can do. But that machine alone cannot provide manufacturers with a competitive edge. Gaining the edge also requires you to reorient your manufacturing process—and maybe other departments as well—to take full advantage of the opportunities offered by the new technology.

5

Global Forces

Let's say you walk into a restaurant in Hartford, Connecticut, and order a bottle of Kirin, a popular Japanese beer. Protectionists would say this is another example of an American consumer sending dollars to Japan. But the truth is not quite so simple.

The glass bottle you're drinking out of was probably manufactured by Yamamora Glass, located just outside Tokyo. But the machines that made the glass bottles in Japan were assembled at Emhart's glass-machinery factory in Sweden. And the parts for the glass-manufacturing machine were themselves manufactured all over the world—in Switzerland, in Singapore, and even at a plant in Windsor, Connecticut, just a few miles from where you're now sipping your beer.

You may be drinking Japanese beer, but you're holding a global bottle. Your purchase of the beer isn't just sending money to Japan: It's part of a complex international economic chain that affects the profitability of many companies all over the world, including one in your own backyard. Given the number of countries involved in manufacturing the glass bottle for Kirin, the idea that any product could be classified as foreign or domestic seems provincial.

Whether final manufactured products themselves are imported or domestic, the manufacturing processes and machines that go into the products themselves almost always have multinational origins. Thus, the manufacturer of any product—even a domestic product for domestic purchase—is frequently affected by global forces far beyond its control. Political events affect the availability of raw materials. Currency rates and foreign tariffs and regulations can affect the price of machinery. And wage rates, governmental policy, technological advances, and even just shrewd thinking by business executives in other countries can precipitate a foreign invasion that turns U.S. markets upside down. In short, the global economy, like rapid technological advancement, is an agent of change manufacturers must respond to—and harness to their advantage.

As with technology, the importance of these global forces affecting manufacturing is more subtle than it appears at first. Thinking globally does not mean simply opening up foreign markets or defending against foreign invaders, any more than using technology wisely means simply buying a machine. For manufacturing executives everywhere—whether in Singapore or in Windsor, Connecticut—global competition, just like technology, requires rethinking of their businesses and what makes them competitive.

There are technological advances to synthesize and political upheavals to follow throughout the world and competition from foreign competitors to monitor. Manufacturing executives must recognize that they all are competing internationally, all the time, for materials, labor, equipment, and customers. In short, the rules of the game have changed.

Even executives at so-called multinational corporations are confronted with the problems generated by global forces. In the past, multinationals have operated a series of divisions in different countries, manufacturing products domestically in those nations for purchase there. Now they must recognize that country-specific divisions can be affected by global forces and global competitors.

As with the other areas of change, the challenge of thinking globally can be a minefield for those who are trapped in antiquated ways of thinking. But for a forward-looking manager or executive, global business means opportunity.

The Battle at Home

Businesses in the United States have felt global forces most acutely through the sudden appearance of formidable foreign competitors in their domestic markets. This invasion is one reason for the considerable discussion among politicians about whether to curtail free trade—that is, to impose quotas and restrictions on foreign products as a way of protecting jobs and companies.

But U.S. manufacturing companies seeking to defend their turf cannot rely exclusively on protectionist sentiment: Foreign success here is not due exclusively to management and political trends in other countries. It has come about in large part because of changes in the American consumer—changes that are not likely to go away no matter what happens to U.S. trade laws.

In the past three decades, two extremely important changes that have allowed foreign competitors to gain a foothold in the United States: (1) The retail distribution system has become much more centralized, making it easier for a foreign company to place its products on U.S. shelves; and (2) the American consumer has become much less nationalistic, first shifting brands because of price and later becoming loyal customers of foreign manufacturers. Let's examine each of these changes in detail.

Distribution used to be a major challenge to any manufacturer entering the U.S. market. Even if a company had a product that Americans probably would buy at a price they wanted to pay, it wasn't easy to figure out how to get that product into every corner store in the country. And until a generation or so ago, the corner store was where Americans bought their products—whether it was the corner toy store for teddy bears or the corner hardware store for hammers and nails.

Today the corner store is virtually gone. In hardware, for example, large specialized chains have emerged, and department stores such as Sears and Penney's have begun to capture a significant share of the hardware market as well. These large retail chains make large-scale purchases of hardware products and therefore serve as the distribution system for the manufacturer. And they rarely are concerned about whether that manufacturer is foreign or domestic; they generally look at only price and quality of the product.

As foreign companies have gained a foothold in this way, they also have invaded U.S. trade shows and established training and service systems in the United States. Corporate executives who believe they are immune from foreign competition on the store shelves are deluding themselves.

Furthermore, once their products are actually on the shelves, foreign competitors have shrewdly captured market share with low prices and then kept it by building brand loyalty. The huge success of discount stores has facilitated this process by fostering an off-price consciousness in the American consumer, who usually selects the lowest price among comparable items without regard to where the product was made. Thus, Americans hold Sony and RCA and, Fuji and Kodak, in equal esteem.

This process does not take place only in the retail arena. In many cases, foreign competitors have used off-brand consciousness to break the domestic manufacturers' stranglehold on business products, which have become an enormous part of our economy. Consider, for example, Xerox's experience with high-end copiers.

When Xerox introduced its top-of-the-line 914 office copier, the company also decided to deemphasize the low end of the market. The lease of large office copiers produced big profits because the lease payments were tied to the number of copies made, and large copiers were used for a huge number of copies. By contrast, desktop copiers produced low profit margins and were not used for significant numbers of copiers. So by the mid-1970s Xerox was virtually ignoring them.

That opened the door for the Japanese companies such as Canon to begin moving into the desktop copier business. Then two things happened that Xerox hadn't anticipated. First, because desktop copies were cheap, office workers began making more copies, and the desktop market expanded. More important, however, when desktop-copier offices grew, they bought large machines—and they bought them from Japanese companies because brand loyalty had developed. By ignoring the low-end market, Xerox was losing the market share of the high-profit machines it had specifically decided to pursue.

This kind of foreign competition in the domestic market is here to stay. It is not going to disappear because of tariffs, quotas, or other trade restrictions. As long as these forces make economic entry into the U.S. market relatively easy, politicians will continue to feel pressure from consumers to let the foreign competitors in—U.S. manufacturing companies must confront global forces head on.

The Global Marketplace

To do so, they must begin to think globally, even if they do not have global aspirations. Even if they see themselves as exclusively domestic, they must understand the global forces that can affect their suppliers, their sources of raw material, and their markets.

For many companies, this means undertaking a global intelligence-gathering effort. Many subscribe to economic and political assessment services, which assist them in monitoring events around the world. Even a domestic company in a competitive industry must keep abreast of a remarkably broad array of concerns: political stability in other countries, currency and debt problems, labor relations, and even foreign government involvement in industry.

These global forces can affect a domestic company in subtle and indirect ways that are easy to overlook. For example, most U.S. manufacturing executives are able to monitor the Japanese government's method of targeting a particular industry and funneling resources into that industry until it cracks foreign markets successfully. But how many are able to track other foreign countries with their eyes on U.S. markets or manufacturing and research jobs? How many U.S. manufacturers, for example, know that the United Kingdom's Department of Industry funds programs for development of industrial robots and flexible manufacturing—actually subsidizing private industry in the very areas of advanced technology that an industrialized, high-wage country such as the United Kingdom (or the United States) must become proficient in to retain manufacturing?

Under this program, the United Kingdom granted over $400,000 to Tucker Fasteners, an Emhart subsidiary with a plant in Birmingham, England. That subsidy influenced Emhart's decision to conduct the project in the United Kingdom, rather than the United States or elsewhere, meaning that U.S. manufacturing jobs as well as research jobs are at risk. But just as important, it placed all U.S. rivet makers at a disadvantage because Tucker doesn't have to bear the full-cost burden of research that will improve the efficiency of its plant. The Birmingham plant is getting new technology at a discount, while U.S. companies have to pay the full freight.

It's not likely that U.S. rivet makers would think to pay close attention to what the United Kingdom's Department of Industry is doing. Yet Tucker's cut-rate technological advance could blindside them unless they're seeking worldwide intelligence closely and planning how to combat foreign attacks being mounted against them.

Direct foreign competition of goods is not the only danger, however. The worldwide flow of capital and currency has accelerated at a frenzied a pace in recent years and carries with it other potential problems that can play a profound role in any manufacturing company's success, even if the company is not directly affected. Take currency shifts, for example. National currency values are not fixed in relation to each other; they float, depending on supply and demand. At first glance, it seems as though a domestic company manufacturing products for domestic consumption would be totally unaffected by shifts in currency relationships. Yet this is not so. Currency shifts can help or harm any company that relies on foreign capital, suppliers, markets, or raw materials or faces competition from a foreign company. And today, almost all U.S. industrial companies fit that description.

In recent years, for instance, the price of Japanese products in the United States has risen far more quickly than the cost of manufacturing those products in Japan. Between 1982 and 1985 hourly compensation for Japanese production workers rose 3.8 percent, but because the yen has risen in value compared to the dollar, the dollar equivalent of a Japanese worker's compensation rose almost 50 percent in that same period. That means the Japanese must significantly increase the U.S. price of their products in order to support even a small wage increase in Japan. If you are a U.S. manufacturer competing in the domestic market against Japanese companies, that's unexpected good news.

Currency shifts can slice both ways, however—and the damage can be fatal if a company has not prepared for the contingency. A good example is the Farrel Company, a Connecticut firm that manufactures chemical polymer processing equipment. Throughout the seventies Farrel's so-called Banbury mixer—the workhorse of polymer processing—placed the company ahead of its competition.

In the 1980s, however, the dollar rose in value compared to the West German deutsche mark, giving Farrel's West German competitors a sudden price advantage. Though there was little technical difference in the type of mixing provided by the mixers from the two countries, Farrel found itself consistently underbid around the globe by German competitors. No amount of cost reductions or productivity gains could offset the problems created by the strong dollar. By the time the dollar began to fall, in the mid-1980s, Farrel had lost a significant portion of its market share to German competitors. Because German brand loyalty had developed, Farrel seemed unlikely to get it back by any means. And Farrel's experience with the currency situation was by no means unique. It occurred in many similar industries, causing U.S. manufacturers to drop from market leadership.

Because Farrel competed worldwide for price-sensitive customers, the company should have been prepared for the possibility that world currency fluctuations would place it at a disadvantage sooner or later. Several steps could have been taken to determine its sensitivity to currency shifts and prepare for that contingency.

For example, any manufacturing process where labor is a higher-than-average percentage of the cost of manufacturing is highly vulnerable to changes in the currency situation. Any company that uses such manufacturing processes had better be ready with alternatives, such as finding a less expensive source that can be used in an emergency or taking steps to improve automation and bring flexible manufacturing systems into the factories. One of the hidden advantages of automation is that it makes U.S. plants much less dependent on conditions beyond their control, such as the cost of labor and currency shifts that might affect the relative value of that cost on a worldwide basis. Furthermore, flexible manufacturing systems permit sudden and dramatic changes to be made in factory output if a quick change in currency relationships alters a company's competitive balance.

In some cases it might even be desirable to find an emergency source and also introduce flexible manufacturing. With a flexible manufacturing system, Farrel might have been able to switch the production of certain parts from a country where currency exchange rates are working against the company to a different location, where the currency situation might be more favorable. Emhart's glass-machinery group has developed this flexibility by placing manufacturing plants in Sweden, the United States, and Singapore, allowing it to respond to currency shifts by shifting orders from one plant to another. For some companies, it might even be desirable to do business overseas with a U.S. company so the transaction could be taken care of completely in dollars. Some observers of real estate markets predict the Japanese may soon use this approach in the United States, with Japanese real estate developers hiring Japanese construction companies to build buildings here, so the transactions may be conducted completely in yen.

Currency fluctuations are only one example of how global thinking must be applied to every factor that has the potential to disrupt operations or harm a company's competitiveness. Most companies should identify alternate sources of materials in case the flow of those materials ever ceases or becomes too expensive to maintain.

Understanding global forces affecting one's business is important, but it is not enough. In order to take full advantage of the opportunities presented around the world, U.S. manufacturing companies also must be prepared to implement global *marketing* strategies—action plans that open foreign markets and don't always fight a war of retreat in the domestic market.

Global Marketing Strategies

The global strategy must build on—or create—a company's unique strengths vis-à-vis global forces and foreign competition. These strengths can include innovative products, service and distribution advantages, and advanced technology. The global strategy is always visionary and often bold, meant to leapfrog the competition in a dramatic way. (This, of course, means it may not always reach the company's financial hurdle rate—another reason financial analysis must ac-

count for the true value of strategically important investments in manufacturing.) The strategy of any particular
company depends on whether it seeks to maintain current
markets domestically or expand into markets throughout the
globe, but they generally fall into three categories—defense,
offense, and global integration.

Defense

Here's an example of a bold move in the face of foreign
competition: When Henry B. Schacht, chairman of Cummins Engine, was faced with the possibility of Japanese competition for his two biggest truck engine customers, he immediately cut prices by 30 percent. Then he tried to figure
out how to cut costs by the same figure. Schacht's goal was
defensive—to preserve market share at all costs in order to
block Japanese entry into the U.S. market.

In fact, the *New York Times* reported in 1987 that Cummins had managed to cut costs by 15 percent—half its goal—
through a series of techniques that I have described elsewhere in this book, including a reduction in the number of
parts used in the engines. But the point is that Cummins
saw the problem as protecting its market share. Contrast that
response with RCA's response twenty-five years ago to the
invasion of Japanese televisions (described in Chapter 2).
Instead of seeking to protect its market share, RCA surrendered the low end of the market to the Japanese and profited
handsomely—in the short-run—by licensing television technology to Japanese companies. A quarter-century later,
Cummins rightly saw that no threat of foreign competition
should be underestimated.

Offense

A defensive move may be a good first step, but it is rarely
enough to permanently defuse the threat of foreign com-

petition. Sometimes a daring offensive move into the competitor's own market is required.

For example, Japanese mainframe computer giants such as Fujitsu and Hitachi have never been able to crack the U.S. market on their own. Why? Because a long time ago, IBM decided that the best defense was a good offense and moved to establish itself in the Japanese market. Today, as a result of that offensive move, IBM holds 25 percent of the Japanese mainframe market—meaning Fujitsu and Hitachi can't generate enough cash at home to mount an assault in the United States. In fact, Fujitsu entered into a joint venture with TRW in the United States partly to finance the fight with IBM back in Japan.

The key here is that the aggressive foreign competitor most likely needs a highly profitable operation back home in order to finance a move into your market. If you move into his market, you are in effect cutting him off from the capital he needs to move into your market.

Of course, foreign countries (particularly the Japanese) don't always provide a level playing field for competitors from foreign countries such as the United States. Still, it is sometimes possible to gain a foothold in a foreign market by exploiting loopholes in protectionist laws and in so doing keep foreign competitors out of your market by forcing them to do battle with you at home. In the seventies the Japanese were restricted throughout Europe to selling small-screen televisions. But these restrictions did not prohibit Japan from supplying pictures tubes, so the Japanese exploited economies of scale by selling picture tubes inexpensively all over the world, including Europe. Furthermore, they could skirt the protectionist measures by manufacturing in Europe and simply found local joint-venture partners, selling European-made televisions under Japanese brand names.

Thomson, France's leading electronics manufacturer, recently acquired RCA's consumer products division from General Electric. The move may indicate that Thomson is ready to do battle with the Japanese companies in the European television market. But no matter what protectionist laws may be on the books, Japan's commanding lead in Europe will keep Thomson confined to markets there, meaning the Japanese will not have to worry about competition from Thomson at home or in the United States.

Global Integration

Caterpillar Tractor Company is the world's dominant manufacturer of construction equipment—and it has a strong presence almost everywhere on the globe. Why? Caterpillar once got a lucky break, and the company was shrewd enough to take maximum advantage of that opportunity.

Following World War II, U.S. Navy Seabees left Caterpillar equipment scattered in nations throughout the world. But instead of forgetting about their foreign Cats at a time when only the U.S. market seemed promising, the company realized that emerging governments and businesses would use them and would need repairs, spare parts, and replacements. So Caterpillar established independent dealerships all over the world to service these abandoned fleets. The dealerships used the profits from the flow of spare parts into these distant locations to pay for the inventorying of new Caterpillar equipment, which was subsequently sold to the enthusiastic foreign owners of the Cats. The dealerships have been profitable since the beginning, establishing a unique and strong global sales and service network.

Then Caterpillar went one step further. The company did most of its major assembly work in the United States, but it also established plants throughout the world—in Europe, Japan, Brazil, Australia—to add local product features. It thereby avoided the high cost of transporting the end products and also became an active and willing participant in local economies around the world. As Thomas Hout, Michael E. Porter, and Eileen Rudden pointed out in their 1982 *Harvard Business Review* article, ''How Global Companies Win

Out,'' ''No single 'world model' was forced on the customer, yet no competitor could match Caterpillar's production and distribution cost.''

Caterpillar had integrated global needs with its own capabilities to create a high value-added product—a product, in fact, that had a great deal of value added to it through its global operation. Though Caterpillar was lucky to have the opportunity created by the Seabees, its strategy was far more sophisticated than mere defense or offense.

The integration approach builds on an earlier offensive or defensive move. Once a company such as Caterpillar is established globally on the sales side, it then can consolidate its gains by using the global network to advantage, offering something no one else has. Something similar occurred with Emhart's global glass-machinery group. As the Caterpillar example proves, spare parts and the ability to retrofit old equipment is extremely important in maintaining a global business. Not only does Emhart have spare-parts depots in Europe and Singapore—so they need not be shipped from the United States—but the company has also developed state-of-the-art ''retrofit kits'' so that glass companies all over the world can easily retrofit old equipment with the latest advances.

The companies described in this chapter—whether they have undertaken offensive, defensive, or integrative moves— all understand that they are operating in a global marketplace. They also recognize that in such a marketplace, thoughtfully and efficiently run manufacturing plants can provide a competitive edge—by taking maximum advantage of opportunities provided by technology and taking bold steps that may transcend traditional financial analysis. Furthermore, as the next chapter shows, it also may require unusual partnerships—partnerships that may have been considered illegal or unethical a generation ago but that have become necessary today by frenzied global competition.

Part III

More Than Technology Is Needed

6

Finance

As vice president for research and development at Singer in the late seventies, I witnessed many technological advances in the design and manufacture of sewing machines. I also witnessed many internal debates over when using those technological advances was justified financially. One of those debates—over the purchase of an automated transfer line— taught me a great lesson about the role of financial analysis in manufacturing.

Capital Justification at Singer

Singer's goal was to launch a new industrial sewing machine, a top-of-the-line product with many features and a great deal of sophistication. To do so, the Sewing Products Group sought to construct a multimillion-dollar automated transfer line at its plant in Elizabeth, New Jersey. Such a line transfers sewing machine parts from one work station to another automatically. Though the investment is large, the ultimate savings can be considerable because of the offsetting decline in the cost of labor.

The capital justification document produced by the Sewing Products Group predicted one of the highest financial returns I had ever seen. The payback ratio was large, and all required financial goals were met, including Singer's corporate financial hurdle rate—that is, the minimum return on investment required for approval of a capital project. The capital appropriation was approved, and the automated transfer line was installed in Elizabeth.

At the same time, however, the apparel industry was shifting from the United States to Third World nations, and the demand for industrial sewing machines shifted as well. Inexpensive machines with fewer features and less sophistication were required in Brazil, Korea, and elsewhere. As for those portions of the apparel industry that remained in the United States and Western Europe, the rapidly changing demands of the fashion world required flexible, low-volume machines. The new Singer machines lacked the ability to reach either end of the market, and they didn't sell.

As a result, the automated lines in Elizabeth usually ran at less than 30 percent of anticipated volume, which meant all the overhead for the capital investment had to be absorbed by only 30 percent of the sewing machines the company had originally anticipated manufacturing, driving unit cost sky high and significantly reducing profit margin. The transfer line never paid for itself.

Singer's justification documents were excellent, but they saw none of this coming. Cost savings on recommended equipment were carefully documented, but all they dealt with was the question of whether the transfer line would pay for itself if a certain sales volume was met. They didn't address the strategic question of whether the demand for the machines would continue and whether the transfer line would help Singer meet the changing demands of the marketplace.

Clearly, the automated transfer line should never have reached the stage where it was proposed as a capital appropriation. Had Singer's industrial marketing organization recognized the global shifts in the marketplace, the company might have taken a different course. The fixed technology of the automated transfer line was useful only if standardized products were manufactured in huge quantities. By contrast, a flexible automation system—facilitating manufacture of many different types of sewing machines—might have better assisted the company in keeping up with the marketplace.

But the justification method wasn't capable of raising that sort of strategic corporate issue: It measured a proposal against financial objectives. The justification method assumed that markets would be stable and growing, even though stability and growth had disappeared from the scene. Yet it was the *only* method Singer used to determine whether to purchase expensive pieces of capital equipment. In other words, the justification system was used in the corporate suite the way robotics are sometimes used on the factory floor—as a panacea rather than simply as a useful tool.

The Game of Number Crunching

Far too often financial analysis in manufacturing operations means only one thing—cost avoidance. Anything that helps a company avoid costs is good; anything that forces a company to incur costs is bad. Again, this approach stems from a corporate attitude that places little strategic value on a robust manufacturing operation. A company's competitive positioning in the world of manufacturing is not regarded as an issue.

Though this narrow financial attitude is probably most pronounced with regard to the justification process, it also pervades many other aspects of U.S. manufacturing, where financial gamesmanship is often more important than market success.

Indeed, a remarkable aspect of corporate financial analysis today is not what it *does* measure but what it *doesn't* measure. For example, the potential profitability of a manufactured product can be destroyed by imprecise cost accounting, even though almost any factory has the means to measure product cost precisely. And financial justification almost never takes into account the cost of handling and storing raw materials and partly finished parts within the factory. It usually concentrates on the cost of labor and capital expenditures. Yet parts in a factory sit idle 98 percent of the time and interact with labor or equipment only 2 percent of the time. This attitude has contributed greatly to a tunnel vision that views manufacturing as a series of discrete pieces and not as a total system.

Finance, like technology, is not an end in itself in manufacturing. It is a tool to be used in achieving strategic success. Thus, to be useful, financial analysis cannot become caught up in a narrow game of number crunching and cost reduction. It must deal with its subject matter broadly and in strategic terms.

For this reason, financial analysis must be able to measure not just a reduction in cost, but literally anything that can improve the efficiency of a factory or improve the profitability of a product. In certain industries, a piece of equipment or an organizational process that can cut a product's development time in half is worth far more to a company than the savings realized by not investing in that equipment or that organizational process.

Texas Instruments was once a leading manufacturer of computer equipment, but according to one former executive, the company took eighteen months to develop new products—an eternity in high-tech product terms—and the product collapsed. By contrast, Compaq has become a leading computer manufacturer by cutting the product development cycle to only nine months—adding nine highly profitable months to the sales potential of its products. Traditional financial analysis, however, would probably not recognize the value of those extra nine months. In a world where competitive position is often just as important as the bottom line, financial analysis must find a way to measure not just the cost of an investment in labor and capital, but that investment's strategic value, as well as the risk associated with making (or not making) that investment.

Financial Analysis for Strategic Goals

I don't believe we should toss out our tried-and-true justification systems and other tools of financial analysis. We still need them to help us understand when an opportunity is worth the cost involved. But I do believe we must update these methods of financial analysis to reflect a sophisticated understanding of what those opportunities and costs really are. In particular, we must recognize that some costs and activities further strategic corporate goals with regard to manufacturing, while others are really tactical decisions designed to keep the company on a steady course. Financial analysis must be used differently in these different situations.

I believe that three areas deserve considerable attention from financial analysts and manufacturing executives who participate in furthering strategic corporate goals: justification systems, product cost accounting, and the true cost of materials handling. Though the justification process provides the most vivid example of narrow financial analysis versus broad strategic thinking, all three areas hold important lessons about the role finance can play in reviving U.S. manufacturing.

Justification Systems

Justification systems such as the one I saw at Singer are the heart of corporate financial analysis. They are, in essence, the screening processes that measure proposals for capital investment against the company's expected return on investment.

The ROI is generally reduced to a single, companywide

index known as the hurdle rate. This single hurdle rate, derived in most cases from the company's cost of capital, is the return that any capital investment must exceed in order to gain approval from the top corporate brass. It is usually measured in the form of other costs saved. Thus, in the case of Singer's transfer line, the capital cost of the automated line was measured against the reduction in labor cost brought about by the new machine's use. (Of course, when Singer failed to sell enough sewing machines to keep its assembly line running at full capacity, the estimated savings in labor cost was greatly reduced because human workers could not work only part-time in such a situation because of labor contracts. Thus, the company was stuck with a capital expense and little offsetting labor savings.)

The hurdle rate has long been controversial, particularly among my colleagues in manufacturing, who believe that modernization or improvement of their plants and equipment is frequently blocked by number crunchers and their hurdle rate. These manufacturing advocates have proposed many alternatives in hopes of breaking the grip the hurdle rate has held on their plants. They have proposed lowering or eliminating the rate, substituting strategic justification for financial justification, and applying different hurdle rates in different situations.

Furthermore, the hurdle rate intertwines with compensation policies that reward short-term performance to make life even more difficult for manufacturing managers. These managers often recognize sooner than anyone else that a piece of capital equipment—or, indeed, an entire manufacturing process—must be replaced. But capital equipment reduces an operating unit's financial performance in two ways. Because it is counted as an asset, it reduces a unit's return on assets. And the value of new capital equipment depreciates quickly, so it reduces the operating profit because the depreciation is figured on the unit's profit-and-loss statement.

Since most company bonus plans rely on these two ratios, division managers are placed in a no-win situation. If they modernize an obsolete plant, they risk losing their yearly bonus. This discourages them from fighting hard for an innovative piece of capital equipment that, though it might be marginal against the hurdle rate, could be essential to the company's long-term prosperity.

After thirty-five years in the trenches, fighting for capital funds in order to develop new products and processes, I have come to this conclusion: We should not fight over whether to raise or lower the hurdle rate or whether to keep it or eliminate it. Continuing to discuss these ideas will only perpetuate manufacturing management's obsession with the hurdle rate, which is often a convenient excuse to ignore more basic problems at the plant.

Instead of endlessly debating where the hurdle rate should be, we should refocus our energies and understand that not all capital investments can be measured against the same index. Not all capital investments have the same kind of impact on a company's future, even if they cost the same amount of money. For example, the hurdle rate may indicate that maintaining a thirty-year-old manufacturing process with new equipment is still the best way to produce a part. But in competitive terms, a manufacturing company probably cannot afford to think that way, no matter what business the company is in.

Fellows Gearshaping, a once-successful maker of equipment used in manufacturing automobile gears, fell into this very trap. Fellows equipment used a mechanical process to chop or carve a gear out of metal. In the seventies Fellows's business grew rapidly because the emergence of the front-wheel drive vehicle drove up the demand for gearshaping. Seeing a market opportunity, Fellows poured enormous capital into new equipment to help cut in half the manufacture time for its traditional products.

But Fellows's analysis of the situation was wrong. The growth in the gearshaping equipment market was temporary. Once the auto manufacturers had purchased equipment for front-wheel-drive gearshaping, demand for Fellows's products returned to normal levels. Furthermore, within a few years Fellows's customers—concerned about the wasted metal in the traditional gearshaping process— were moving toward using molded gears or even toward building engines with no gears at all. When business was good, Fellows had the opportunity to invest in the emerging processes of the future. Instead, because of the financial justification process, it invested heavily in processes that were rapidly becoming obsolete.

To use financial analysis intelligently, managers must learn to understand which investments lend themselves to the justification process and which don't. In the terminology of Harvard Business School professor Gordon Donaldson, we can divide capital investments into two distinct and very different groups—tactical and strategic.

Tactical investments are the capital projects we think of when we think of the hurdle rate. Their overall goal is to continue the business on its existing course, preserving established earnings potential and taking advantage of normal growth within the estimated share of the market. This sort of analysis is most useful when markets are stable and growing; in fact, it is the kind of analysis Detroit's auto companies used when in the fifties and sixties they were virtually unchallenged by imports and could expect the market to grow each year. When the auto companies were challenged by Japanese cars in the seventies, tactical investment analysis served them poorly because growth and stability were no longer characteristics of their market. Likewise, Singer's financial analysis of the automated transfer line, discussed at the beginning of this chapter, served the company poorly by regarding the purchase as a tactical investment when market conditions required a strategic investment.

Strategic investments, on the other hand, are those that, in Donaldson's words, involve ''major changes in the sources of the company's earning power, such as a shift in product mix, technology, market coverage, or share of market. These changes come out of long-range planning or un-expected opportunity and are made at the policy level.'' In other words, strategic investments are the big, bold—and often necessary—investments a company must make to leap ahead of the competition, particularly in the context of to-day's rapidly changing markets and technologies.

Tactical investments, taken as a whole, are sometimes larger in total dollars than strategic investments. And be-cause they cover investments for such areas as equipment replacement, cost savings—usually through labor reduc-tion—and regulatory-related equipment and systems, they are more easily measured against objective financial indices such as the hurdle rate. To put it simply, the corporate ex-ecutives who emerged in the sixties and seventies measured all capital investments as if they were tactical investments *simply because that was an easy way to measure them*—and, as with the auto companies, because markets in the past had been stable and growing.

But the world has changed. Stability and steady growth have been replaced with volatility and unpredictable mar-kets (see Chapter 4). Partly because of the justification sys-tem's bias toward the seemingly cautious strategy of cost avoidance, however, few capital proposals call for dramatic change and improvement in traditional manufacturing pro-cess.

I recently saw a proposal for a system that keeps track of the documentation associated with a product line that has over 50,000 different parts. The proposal was neatly justified financially. But why didn't the division making that proposal rethink the manufacturing process and suggest reducing the number of parts by 50 percent? At a time when companies have little control over the forces that affect them, it might have been a better idea to solve the problem completely when the opportunity presented itself (by reducing the number of parts), rather than simply containing the problem in such a way that keeps the process vulnerable to economic changes in the future (such as a rise in the labor cost of those who keep track of the parts or a competitor that reduces the parts and hence the cost of manufacturing the product). The justification system may or may not recognize the power of such a proposal—but it would vastly improve the company's ability to compete in the marketplace over the long run no matter what the hurdle rate says.

In other words, the justification system *can't* take into account the quantum strategic leap. Inevitably, a company's competitiveness will suffer as a result.

Several rules of thumb can help a manufacturing company rethink its justification process. As with most suggestions in this book, these rules emphasize common sense—taking the big picture into account and thinking through the problem before trying to solve it. Here are three rules of thumb that can help:

1. *Examine the assumptions underlying a justification document.* What does it assume in terms of cost, quality, profitability, market size, market share, competition? Singer learned the hard way that the world of manufacturing has changed dramatically and that assumptions must always be questioned and not taken for granted. The effect of assumptions on the justification document is almost impossible to quantify, so it is a matter of feel: You have to be sure the assumptions are reasonable, given the volatility and unpredictability that characterizes the markets for manufactured goods today.

2. *Don't overlook hidden financial advantages, such as shorter response or development time.* As was explained earlier in the chapter, traditional financial analyses might not account for the true financial benefits of a quantum leap in the speed of product development or responsiveness. These benefits can be difficult to measure, but even when they are intangible, reasonable estimates can be made.

3. *Consider allocating a certain percentage of capital investment to high-growth areas.* This approach can save a lot of internal anguish between the accounting and the manufacturing managers by simply making quantum-leap strategic investments a high priority within the company.

Product Cost Accounting

Some thirty-five years ago, when I was a young engineer just out of MIT, I went to work in RCA's Building Number 10 in Camden, New Jersey. A wide variety of engineering-related products were manufactured in Building Number 10, but all were placed under a single reporting entity. Thus, for example, RCA's industrial inspection equipment was being manufactured in a job shop atmosphere alongside scientific instruments, sound systems for commercial and education institutions, closed-circuit TV systems, and David Sarnoff's favorite RCA product, the electron microscope. All these products were manufactured in the same plant because they shared capital equipment. The system made sense; costs could be conserved and RCA could ensure that the capital equipment would not remain idle.

But what struck me as odd was the company's cost allocation system. Then as now, at most factories, including RCA's, elaborate procedures allocated the cost of direct and indirect labor for each product, as well as the material that went into that product. Many factory managers gleefully pointed out that they knew their labor cost right down to the penny.

Yet allocation of the cost of capital equipment was a different story. Far from being allocated down to the penny, the cost of all capital equipment was shared equally by all product lines using it. Let us say, for example, that five product lines each gross $2 million per year but that one used half of all the capital equipment time, factory space, and energy costs in the factory. Under the RCA system, which would not be unusual even today, the product line that used half the equipment and energy would be charged for only 20 percent of the total overhead. The other four, which used the capital equipment a combined total of 50 percent of the time, would be charged for 80 percent of the overhead.

It quickly became clear to me that in this cost accounting environment, a factory manager could materially affect the cost of one product over another by shifting overhead rates.

For example, many RCA managers felt the cost of the electron microscope was underestimated because it utilized more overhead than other product lines but not more overhead cost. In effect, they insisted, it was being covertly subsidized by other product lines. But since Sarnoff saw the microscope as a great contribution to mankind, RCA's executives had little motivation to find out whether complaints were true.

On the other hand, many managers in RCA's industrial sound products group believed their products bore an unfair share of cost allocations—that, in fact, they were subsidizing other product lines, such as the electron microscope. Partly because of the high cost of manufacturing the products, RCA divested the industrial sound products group. But a big surprise followed: Without the industrial sound products to subsidize their capital costs, other products being manufactured in the same factory experienced significant cost increases.

Had the true (that is, lower) cost of the industrial sound products been known at RCA's headquarters, the company might have retained and nurtured them and enhanced its own profitability in the process. Had the true (that is, higher) cost of the electron microscope been revealed, David Sarnoff might still have insisted on its development—but at least the cost of RCA's desire to assist mankind would have been made clear, not buried in the cost of industrial sound products or some other line.

Cost accounting systems were designed decades ago to meet the needs of much simpler organizations. In those days, each company made only a few product lines—or even just one. Manually calculating the amount of resources used by each product was difficult at best, and the significant cost factor was labor, not overhead. In management's view, labor cost was so dominant that overhead was estimated in relation to it. For example, one dollar in direct labor translated reliably into two or three dollars in overhead.

Over time, however, conditions changed. As the number

of product lines using the same equipment increased, and as products became more specialized, so did their use of the capital equipment. For a long time, however, information technology did not allow accurate data collection on how this equipment was used. As manufacturing companies grew, finished products were often the result of manufacturing and assembly at several other plants within the same company. Since each of the plants was considered a profit center, an interplant markup was included in the product cost and eliminated in consolidation—making accurate cost accounting even more difficult.

Even more important, however, was the changing relationship between labor and overhead. Every new piece of capital equipment further decreased labor costs, driving the ratio further and further apart and making the relationship meaningless. Furthermore, under antiquated overhead allocation policies, it was not unusual to see products absorb the cost of a new piece of equipment even if they were not manufactured on it.

More than thirty years ago, when RCA divested the industrial sound products group, it was readily apparent to me that imprecise cost accounting could harm corporate decision making. But today the stakes are much higher. Decisions to make a product, buy a product line from another company, or decide to outsource assembly foreign companies are all tremendously important strategic decisions that can make or break a manufacturing company. Remarkably enough, they often are made with incomplete or even erroneous cost data. Given the competitive pressures of today's world, manufacturing companies cannot succeed if they have only a vague idea of how much their products cost.

Furthermore, today precise product cost accounting *is* possible, thanks to techniques pioneered by some industries, such as pharmaceuticals, which for their own reasons have had to hold themselves to a rigorous standard. After my experience with cost accounting at RCA and other manufacturing companies, for example, I was startled by what I found when I went to work at the pharmaceutical firm of Merck & Company, now known as Merck Sharpe & Dohme.

The Merck factory was a sprawling array of buildings on the border of the two New Jersey towns of Rahway and Linden. Each individual building produced a different pharmaceutical product. Building 121 produced streptomycin, building 10 produced penicillin, and so on. Even the raw materials used in each of Merck's final product plants were produced separately. For example, Oleum, a strong sulfuric acid, was produced all by itself in Building 72.

Each building was equipped with the instrumentation necessary to monitor every ounce of raw material that went into each process. Raw materials weighed in and final product weighed out. Just as carefully monitored were steam, water, electricity, gas, and even air (air often had to be supercleaned).

Each plant had its own dedicated personnel, including chemical engineering support and indirect and direct labor. When a maintenance person from Merck's central maintenance group entered any specific building, a work-order slip was immediately issued. Even the waste leaving each building was carefully monitored for quantity, pH, and contents to ensure effective sewage disposal—and to allocate those disposal charges to the processes accurately.

In short, Merck's management had an in-depth understanding of all product costs, from labor right down to the lights. In part, Merck, like other chemical and pharmaceutical companies, kept careful track of its materials because they can be hazardous and should not be erroneously mixed together. But Merck's system proves that the methods and technology are available for any business to keep close track of product costs.

With computer-integrated manufacturing equipment, the data that command and control operations can also be used to measure continuously the use of resources and the quantity and quality of output. For example, it's no longer necessary to estimate the time a part spends in various operations throughout a factory. The information is readily available—and not just monthly or quarterly but instantaneously. It's not necessary to wait until the middle of September to get the factory cost report for August. This allows daily or even hourly changes to handle problems or take advantage of opportunities that arise suddenly.

Finally—and most important—modern data bases at last make it possible for factories to move away from outdated cost accounting systems based on direct labor. With the overhead burden rate in relation to direct labor reaching 400 to 500 percent in most industries—1,000 to 2,000 percent in a highly automated environment—direct labor is no longer a useful yardstick.

Once again, the solution lies not so much in acquiring fancy technological or financial tools but in understanding what they should be used for. In the case of product cost accounting, information that could be used to help make a manufacturing plant more competitive is easily available but virtually ignored. Plant managers are comfortable with the traditional techniques, and their corporate bosses do not see the strategic value of sophisticated methods. Like most other aspects of U.S. manufacturing, product cost accounting can be a valuable competitive tool—but only if corporate financial analysts believe factories are strategically important to their companies and therefore worth the time and effort it takes to take maximum advantage of the opportunities new technology provides.

Materials Handling

In most manufacturing operations, financial analysis concentrates almost exclusively on capital and labor. How should a plant's costs be allocated among its different products? Can a new piece of capital equipment save enough money in labor to be worth purchasing? Can a new machine improve productivity by accelerating the pace of the actual manufacturing work?

In addition to drawbacks that I have pointed out, these questions contain another hidden weakness as well: They attack only part of the problem. True cost savings and improved efficiency, which are so important to renewed manufacturing competitiveness, cannot be attained in the factory unless parts and materials are handled and stored far more efficiently than they are now.

According to the Society of Manufacturing Engineers, a part in a factory spends an average 5 percent of its time sitting on the machine itself; the other 95 percent of the time it is moving or being stored. Furthermore, during the time that it *is* on the machine, it sits idle 60 percent of the time and is worked on only 40 percent of that time.

Thus, a metal part in a factory lays idle 98 percent of the time. Knowing this fact can change a manager's entire attitude toward cost-saving and financial expenditure. Many manufacturing engineers, for example, believe that the manufacturing organization's productivity should be improved by increasing the machine-cutting speed. But to do so attacks only 2 percent of the problem. Applying great effort and expense still results in 98 percent of the problem remaining untouched. To concentrate on labor or on capital improvements will always be an uphill battle.

The true cost of such inefficiency within the factory is remarkably high. Not long ago I learned that part of the reason the textile industry is a weak link in U.S. manufacturing is because of the remarkable inefficiency of our textile factories. A fiber's journey from the chemical fiber plant where it is produced, through the garment manufacturing process, and into the customer's hand as part of a shirt can take up to sixty *weeks*. For well over a year, that fiber spends the vast majority of its time between machine operations sitting in storage space.

The textile industry moved from New England to the non-unionized South and from there to Asia almost entirely because of the cost of labor. But it's easy to see that labor represents only a small part of the economic competitiveness problem in this industry. If U.S. textile factories made even minor improvements in efficiency in materials handling, they could achieve cost-cutting inside the factory that would keep textile jobs in the United States.

One company that has made strides in this area is Xerox, which recognized materials handling as a major financial problem at its plant in Fremont, California. As Xerox won a large share of the computer printer market in the seventies, the Fremont plant grew rapidly, eventually spreading into thirteen buildings. But that arrangement placed the Fremont plant at a strategic disadvantage.

According to *Manufacturing Engineering* magazine, Xerox completely reorganized the factory to make materials handling more efficient. The plant now has 800 feet of conveyor belts to move work in progress. An integrated computer system tracks production electronically; every part that enters the factory is marked with a bar code. The automated system has eliminated 800,000 sheets of paper per year, and the factory has cut production time by 66 percent and work-in-progress inventory by 50 percent. Materials handling labor has been cut 80 percent and overhead has been cut 10 to 30 percent. Overall savings to the company: $30 million per year. In traditional financial analysis, Xerox's cost of materials handling probably would be overlooked, as would the imprecision in product cost and the financial opportunities presented by strategic investment.

Flaws of traditional financial analysis require us to better understand the role financial analysis can play in helping manufacturers compete in a fast-paced, worldwide market. Yes, we must quantify our goals and justify our investments financially. But we cannot do so based on assumptions about the way the world of U.S. manufacturing was twenty years ago. We must do so with our eyes open, in full knowledge that technology on the one hand, and the emergence of global competition on the other, have changed the rules of the game.

7

External Relationships

If you had to name the five fiercest competitors in the glass-container business, you'd probably select Rockware Glass and Brockway from the United States, Wiegand Glass from West Germany, Yamamura Glass of Japan, and ACG of Australia. Ten years ago, you probably wouldn't have been able to get them all in the same room together—assuming the U.S. Department of Justice would have allowed the meeting at all.

Yet today, these five competitors—along with Emhart, the world's leading manufacturer of glass-container machinery—are partners. Three years ago, they formed the International Partnership for Glass Research and embarked on a crash program to create a new glass container only half the weight and ten times stronger than the ones made now.

The reason for this unlikely partnership is simple. For 4,000 years, glass containers dominated the marketplace. But since 1980, glass has been steadily losing ground to plastic. Though they're still competitors, the six glass container companies recognized the advantage of joining together to fight a mutual enemy.

Separately, no single company had the research capacity to identify possible technical opportunities, let alone achieve the targeted increase in glass strength. But together they are much stronger. Through IPGR's technology board, funds are distributed to outside organizations for such projects as laser-flash reheating to heal cracks during glass production; the application of solgel solutions that have been used in making glass for telescope lenses and microscopes; and the adaption of recent advances in ceramics to glass manufacturing. Even if the ultimate target is not reached, we can be fairly certain that the consortium will still produce significant advances in the glassmaking process—advances that would not have come about otherwise.

Cross-Breeding, Not In-Breeding

IPGR is a good example of a troubled industry that recognizes that to survive, it must encourage cross-breeding, not in-breeding. Throughout this book, I have emphasized my belief that traditional approaches to manufacturing—the idea of keeping the machines humming—have undermined U.S. industry. To remain competitive, U.S. manufacturing companies must go beyond the four walls of their factories in order to broaden their view of the world and find the resources necessary to move ahead. That means they must form partnerships—with governments, with universities, and even, as IPGR suggests, with competitors. They must move in this direction because they are being confronted with at least four forces they have never witnessed before:

1. As new technology becomes more expensive to develop and produce, the financial resources required to provide the critical mass for research is spiraling beyond the means of any single company. For example, a U.S. Commerce Department analysis recently found that international competitiveness in the use of robotics must involve, for some industries, cooperative ventures. The resources required are too great for even the largest companies.
2. High-tech companies can no longer invest in just a few

products and keep up a string of innovations. Several high-technology sectors are converging—telecommunications and computers, for example. Companies must have access to a broader range of technological skill.

3. Because of manufacturing's reputation as a backwater of U.S. business, the talent required to achieve future breakthroughs is becoming scarcer.

4. Time has become the most critical element of all. As product cycles have become shorter, U.S. companies have been forced to compress research and development. The traditional method of spreading out manufacturing developments over time in order to conserve cash clearly won't work any longer.

In my opinion, the traditional manufacturing managers and engineers—though they may have extraordinary experience and skill—are, in many cases, too narrowly focused to meet these challenges alone.

There is no question that a manager or engineer who has gained experience in a cast-iron foundry, for example, has an invaluable background in this field. But think how much better equipped that factory would be if that manager or engineer were in regular contact with people who explore the metallurgy of raw materials or the physics and chemistry of the process. The factory floor alone, however much "street smarts" it might contain, cannot provide the insights needed to propel our factories into the next century.

Nor can our academic institutions alone prepare us for a complex, changing job environment in the future. Only by cross-breeding the two—by bringing manufacturing managers into contact with thinking that reaches far beyond their own company—can U.S. manufacturing rise to the challenge.

Opportunities for Cross-Breeding

There are two major areas of opportunity for cross-breeding that American manufacturing companies must examine: (1)

strategic partnering, such as the joint research institute created by the glass companies; and (2) university/industry programs, including new federal and state initiatives related to
manufacturing.

Strategic Partnering

In 1987 and 1988 the United States saw the emergence of
a remarkable collaborative effort on the part of the semiconductor industry. Threatened by Japanese competition, the
major U.S. semiconductor manufacturers created a consortium called Sematech, a $250-million-a-year organization de-
signed to conduct basic research in semiconductors—quickly
and efficiently, in order to keep ahead of the Japanese. The
member companies take research results and compete with
each other to develop commercial products based on new
technology.

Historically, an organization like Sematech might have
run into antitrust problems with the U.S. Justice Department, but the federal government has been supportive of
Sematech. Congress appropriated $100 million to assist in
its operations, mostly because of potential Pentagon uses for
the new technology. In 1984 President Reagan signed into
law the National Cooperative Research Act, loosening antitrust rules for such cooperative ventures. Now, cooperative
ventures between companies are permissible when such arrangements add to a company's overall efficiency and benefit the society at large. Since the law was passed, some forty
consortia have been organized through the assistance of
Bruce Merrifield, deputy secretary of productivity, technology, and innovation with the U.S. Commerce Department,
which championed the new law.

Like the International Partnership for Glass Research, Sematech and other research consortia are efforts by competitors to band together to advance the interests of an entire
industry. There is, of course, nothing new about the concept

of joint ventures and cooperative arrangements. For years, some form of cooperative research and development has been carried on by trade associations such as the American Iron and Steel Institute and the Electric Power Research Institute, national labs such as Oakridge National Laboratory, and universities. But there is definitely something new about the scope and intent of these efforts.

First, the incentive driving most of these partnerships is not a desire to corner the market but a common, external threat, such as competition from abroad or from other industries. Second, they are strategic arrangements. They allow competitors, potential competitors, and customers to work together to implement a common strategic vision on the one hand, while competing for specific markets on the other. Third, they are designed not just for the long term but to help companies produce immediate results. By collaborating with others, a company can put less money into basic, precommercial research and more money and effort into its own specific commercial application of the research results. Companies can change their focus rapidly and dramatically, as volatile worldwide markets often require, without a major realignment of internal resources.

But industrywide research consortia are not the only form of cooperative venture gaining popularity in industry today. Just as important are individual agreements between two or more companies that might, under different circumstances, be competitors. Though these agreements take many forms, perhaps the most exciting are cooperative ventures between large companies and small ones.

Large, mature companies often have established production plants with an established customer base. But they also often need revitalization and have excess production capacity. On the other hand, smaller, more entrepreneurially oriented firms often develop new products faster and more efficiently than large firms.

A partnership of two such firms has benefits for both. By joining forces with a small firm, a large company can test-market new, high-risk technologies and products without a major commitment of internal resources. And the small companies, though they may fear that the large firm will squeeze them out of the marketplace, also view their larger partner as an enormous potential resource through which to expand their business.

Emhart has established an unusual relationship with Technology Research Company in Danbury, Connecticut. Technology Research is engaged in R&D for robotics in the health care field. Emhart, which is interested in robotics technology, and 3M, which has a strong health care division, provided venture capital to the firm in exchange for a 20 percent equity stake and representation on the board of directors. The arrangement is an advantage for both sides because if Technology Research had come in-house at Emhart, the entrepreneurs would have been pigeonholed and probably wouldn't be as creative or productive as they are now. Emhart has also established Technology Transactions, Incorporated, a venture capital subsidiary funding twenty small companies, including the other 80 percent of Technology Research. Such ventures would never have occurred at Emhart even five years ago.

Similar is the partnership between General Motors and Etak, Incorporated, a California-based manufacturer that developed a computer-controlled navigation system for automobiles. According to a March 1988 issue of *Corporate Venturing News*, when Etak was presenting its system to the auto manufacturers, GM was working on a similar system. But Etak's system was more advanced. Therefore, once market research confirmed consumer interest in the idea, GM signed an exclusive license to manufacture Etak's system in North America.

In the arrangement, GM saves both time and money in developing the system and probably will make a profit on the feature as well. Etak receives up-front capital, future royalties, and, of course, the credibility of being associated with GM.

Particularly where different technologies must be married, two large companies may benefit from an agreement. For example, IBM has entered into partnership with MCI, which provides telecommunications services, and Intel, a semiconductor manufacturer.

Bruce Merrifield, who was the cooperative venture guru of the Commerce Department under President Reagan, believes that eventually, in some cases, a large partner won't be needed for large-scale cooperative projects. He predicts that large and expensive flexible manufacturing systems will be shared by small manufacturing companies, allowing them to compete in price, quality, and timing.

Such shared facilities—now being examined by state governments, incubator centers, and others—could virtually revolutionize some sectors of manufacturing. For one thing, they would create a manufacturing component to the service economy, as small firms lease time on the flexible system, much as they would lease computer time. For another, they would dramatically reduce the strategic advantage large companies enjoy in capital-intensive high-technology industries.

Cooperative ventures of a more traditional type can also be expanded into newly emerging areas to the company's advantage. For example, manufacturing organizations have traditionally relied on vendors for jointly improving a production process. In other situations, manufacturers have brought in consultants to deal with quality assurance, plant layout, and so on.

What's often missing, as our chapter on technology suggested (see Chapter 4), is a systems view of manufacturing— an understanding that automating or improving part of the production process won't help if the total factory environment is ignored. But a new group of companies called systems integrators is emerging to assist in that effort too. These firms frequently have instant expertise that larger companies must acquire.

True Temper Hardware, for example, hired ITI of Cincinnati, Ohio, to help in the design of plastic wheelbarrows. True Temper had decades of experience in designing and manufacturing metal wheelbarrows. But because of its experience in integrating total systems at General Motors factories, ITI had the computer-aided capability to design the dies needed for the plastic wheelbarrows. Without ITI, True Temper would have spent considerable time learning how to design in plastic—and possibly would have relied too heavily on its experience with metals.

At their most ingenious, cooperative agreements can be used in creative combinations to dramatically improve a company's competitiveness. For example, Olivetti, an Italian office-automation equipment company, is a fairly small firm that must butt heads with IBM, Xerox, and other giants. But it has used hook-ups with both large and small firms very deftly. Association with many small entrepreneurial firms has given the company access to the latest technologies and products. It also has an important relationship with AT&T and manufactures some AT&T equipment and markets some AT&T products. Olivetti has two keys it never could have obtained on its own—access to AT&T's vast U.S. distribution network and entrance to the telecommunications market. A recent partnership with Toshiba gave Olivetti access to Toshiba's office automation technology and broadened Olivetti's market base in Japan.

These alliances have helped solidify Olivetti's position at home and abroad, allowing it to become a truly integrated global producer of office automation equipment. Without these alliances, Olivetti would not have been able to attain a strong position throughout the world.

Such cooperative efforts are not always easy or smooth. Lansing Felker, who runs the Commerce Department's Industrial Technologies Program, has identified four ground rules for such efforts:

1. *The companies, not those who perform the research, must set the agenda.* This is not basic research. The companies know what research is really needed to improve competitiveness.

2. *The location of the research should be the last consideration.* The location should serve the needs of the research agenda as it has been determined by the companies.
3. *Top management must be directly involved in setting the agenda.* That way, research will be directly related to long-term business plans.
4. *The price must be high enough to engage top management's attention.* If the company is putting millions of dollars into the cooperative effort, then the top executives will have enough invested in it to make sure it suits their needs.

University/Industry Partnerships

It's only about sixty miles from Emhart's corporate headquarters near Hartford to the Worcester Polytechnic Institute in Massachusetts. But in the case of the Manufacturing Engineering Application Center, that distance proved to be enough to allow a partnership between the two organizations achieve its goal.

One day in the spring of 1984 a bus filled with thirty-three Emhart manufacturing people started up Route 84 out of Hartford, bound for Worcester. The group included manufacturing engineers, shop foremen, a production supervisor, and a union shop steward. Their journey was undertaken to witness a new robotic loading and unloading system, which was being tested at WPI prior to its installation at Emhart's hardware division in Berlin, Connecticut.

On the way to WPI that morning, the people on the bus were apprehensive and full of questions: "What is a robot?" "Tell us how it works." "What is meant by programming a robot?" And jokingly on the surface but seriously underneath, "Will the robot replace us?"

Once in Worcester, the people from the Berlin factory were able to see firsthand exactly what a robot can and cannot do. WPI professors conducted a workshop at which the factory workers were briefed on robotic concepts and given the chance to ask questions. During the day, they discovered that they could cope with the technology of the robot and saw that the robot could load and unload machines safely and eliminate tedious human work. At the end, they each received a certificate from WPI saying they had completed a robotics workshop sponsored by the institute.

The atmosphere on the bus ride home was completely different. Far from apprehensive, the factory workers were jovial. And instead of questions, they had comments. "Is that all it is?" one person asked. "A robot is nothing more than any other piece of automated equipment we use in our factory," another said. "Interestingly, the piece parts still have to be fixtured so robots will still need people like us," said the manufacturing engineers.

The trip to Worcester had worked better than we had hoped. One of our goals in conducting the research project at WPI was to create some distance between Emhart and the project. Factory managers have a long memory for failures on the shop floor. If our new robot had failed on the factory floor, the memory would have lingered for ten years or more, souring the workers to other innovations. If the new robot had failed at WPI, however, the failure would have stopped there. We simply could discontinue the program without having to live with that failure as we moved onto another robotic application. We would not have to deal with lingering memories.

That distance was an important reason that the Emhart-WPI partnership was forged by my predecessor at Emhart, Wally Abel. But it was not the only one. Abel knew he had to move very quickly in developing the robotic technology: His objective was to create active systems in a year or less. Such a timetable would have been impossible on the shop floor, but WPI's faculty and students were delighted to take on short-term application-oriented engineering projects that taught students how to adhere to industrial deadlines.

Subsequently, both parties have gone on to other ventures separately. Emhart has established an internal Center for Technology Innovation, and MEAC, as the WPI center is called, has worked with many other companies, including Digital Equipment Corporation and General Electric. But the fast-track robotics research partnership holds an important lesson: Universities and manufacturing companies both have a great deal to gain from partnerships.

Time, talent, and cost are pushing American companies toward cooperative research, and all play a role in creating the need for university partnerships. But underlying these forces—particularly talent and cost—is manufacturing's reputation as a backwater in U.S. industry where the typical manufacturing manager lives a harried and frustrating life.

The real-life effects of this reputation are sobering: It scares away almost all the good talent from engineering and management schools, and it leads top corporate brass to ignore engineering research even when they pay close attention to product R&D. To counterbalance this image with no outside assistance would require a herculean effort on the part of U.S. manufacturing companies (to say nothing of a swift and remarkable change in corporate culture), but partnerships with universities can help the industrial sector make significant strides in both areas.

Talent. Manufacturing continually fails to attract quality candidates for managerial positions. According to Nam Suh, chief of engineering at the National Science Foundation, more than 200,000 college-degreed engineers work in product-related functions. Less than 2,000 engineers working in manufacturing have degrees.

Even those who are college-educated often have a poor background for manufacturing work. Their education usually is narrowly focused; manufacturing graduates need grounding in academic and laboratory training in electronics, information systems, materials science, advanced materials engineering, and machine dynamics. Also needed—and ignored by universities now—are skills required to identify and analyze new approaches needed, such as simulation, design methodology, systems optimization, and systems integration. Graduates entering manufacturing also lack, but need, basic business skills such as finance, business concepts, decision analysis, and people skills—the latter being among the most important but also most ignored in manufacturing.

Beyond inadequate education and training, manufacturing managerial candidates face the hurdle of the image problem. For both management and engineering prospects, work in manufacturing is seen as too dirty, too poorly compensated, and ultimately too frustrating. In college, they learn almost nothing about the opportunities in U.S. manufacturing today. Thus, the managerial ranks continue to draw people who do not have a college education—people who are shop-wise but lack a broader perspective.

The Massachusetts Institute of Technology, one of the finest technical institutions in the United States, has decided to tackle this problem with its Leaders for Manufacturing program, a joint project of the Sloan School of Management and the School of Engineering. Recognizing that manufacturing "has neither the opportunity nor the glamour of other institutions," MIT has undertaken to realign its own priorities to help solve manufacturing's leadership problem.

One of the program's leading supporters is the Sloan School's dean, Lester Thurow, who is one of the leading economists in the United States and has written widely about the nation's economic ills. Though the program will include a wide range of areas, including expanded research and the participation of industries, its core is a master's degree in management and engineering. In establishing the Leaders for Manufacturing program, MIT has done what many U.S. corporations *should* do: It has recognized that manufacturing is an important strategic tool in worldwide economic competition and given the subject strategic importance within its own curriculum.

As an example of a case where industry, universities, and the state government can join forces together to further manufacturing, consider the computerized plant simulation program conducted by the Threaded Fastener Division of Molly. Molly Fastener Company, located in Temple, Pennsylvania, manufactures a wide variety of fasteners for the industrial, construction, and automotive industries. The consumer knows the company by its tradenamed fastener, the Molly bolt.

The manufacturing of these fasteners requires a number of production operations. The task requires extremely diligent and detailed scheduling in order to realize an overall plant efficiency. With increasing competitive pressures from overseas, Molly has continued to rely on its solid product base, excellent name recognition, and superior design engineering to maintain its position as a world leader in the industry. However, like most U.S. companies, Molly recognizes that it needs a greater edge to maintain and increase its position as the lowest-cost producer and market leader. Philip G. Honsinger, manufacturing manager of Molly, challenged his manufacturing engineers to innovate new ways to improve the manufacturing process.

The complexity of the manufacturing process at Molly can be realized by considering the numbers: Molly can assemble and package at the rate of 15 million pieces per minute. Within this manufacturing environment, it must be able to quickly change plant layout and production schedule to eliminate manufacturing bottlenecks, reduce work-in-process inventory, and optimize equipment utilization and efficiency in less than one afternoon. To help solve these problems, Molly's manufacturing engineers turned to Lehigh University for the development of manufacturing software simulation. Funding for this joint simulation software program between Lehigh University and the Molly Company in Pennsylvania came from state funds through the Ben Franklin Partnership in Pennsylvania.

As a result of the joint Lehigh-Molly partnership, simulation software was developed that gave Molly the ability to mathematically model its manufacturing operations. Through the modeling, Molly could determine the impact of installing a new piece of expensive equipment utilizing the simulation in advance before buying the equipment. The main thrust of the software simulation is optimization; its main benefits are economy and speed. The rationale for the simulation was that it puts information in the form where Molly's engineering managers can make better decisions with respect to plant operations.

When I first saw the results of this program, Honsinger's manufacturing engineers Kerry Kovarik and Jerry Mundhenke demonstrated and simulated alternative manufacturing plant layouts for their operation. Within a few minutes both of these manufacturing engineers were able to grasp many of the concepts that industrial engineers require much time to learn through experience. The software simulation provided these two young manufacturing engineers with the ability to play what-if games and thus to optimize a plant layout. In this particular case the simulation program provided the means by which the Molly plant was able to use existing machinery rather than purchase an expensive piece of capital equipment.

The program represents an example of how a company, Molly, in Temple, Pennsylvania, was able to join forces with Lehigh University and use Pennsylvania state funds through their state Ben Franklin program—thus providing a new tool for factory managers. The tool—factory simulation utilizing artificial intelligence techniques—may not meet all of the expectations that proponents claim for the system. On the other hand, however, Honsinger challenged his manufacturing engineers to study a problem that exists within many companies—namely, to optimize a production line, determine whether a piece of capital equipment will really do the job, and ultimately smooth the production flow. In this case the simulation techniques provided a stimulating tool for engineers and also brought them in contact with Lehigh University, which is well known in the field of computer-integrated manufacturing. In a sense, this particular factory simulation program accelerated the knowledge of two young manufacturing engineers.

The important point here is that many manufacturing managers expect these kinds of tools to answer all of the questions. The simulation software developed by Lehigh for Molly was not a panacea, but the program did provide the tools necessary for two engineers to achieve a better understanding of the shop-floor problem in a relatively shorter period of time.

Engineering Research. Little is known about the amount of money spent on engineering research. But my guess is that if most companies spend 2 to 3 percent of their total revenue on research and development, they spend 0.4 percent or less on engineering research—and that is high for many companies. The truth is that most companies conduct no engineering research at all unless they rely on proprietary automation equipment to manufacture their product.

Part of the reason for this, no doubt, is that establishing an engineering research lab large enough to create a critical mass is expensive. A National Science Foundation study on capital requirements for academic research gives some idea of what that cost is. The start-up cost for a material lab, after accounting for inflation, increased from $825,000 in 1970 to $3.4 million in 1985—an increase of 10 percent per year for fifteen years. And the rate of innovation for laboratory R&D equipment is increasing. Just since 1975, obsolescence time for such equipment has been cut in half, from seven to ten years to three to five years.

Furthermore, this gap is *not* being made up in academia. As a report by the National Academy of Engineering concluded in 1985: "Increasingly, U.S. universities and colleges have been unable to afford the equipment required to provide hands-on experience to engineering students. Thus, engineering education has provided inadequate exposure to the instruments, systems, and processes of modern technology, and there has been a lack of practical experience among graduates."

Engineering Research Centers: A Model Partnership. In recent years, the National Science Foundation—and particularly its engineering section, under the leadership of Nam Suh—has placed great emphasis on the university-industry link in manufacturing. Currently, NSF is in the process of designating eighty Engineering Research Centers, which will generate a vast amount of basic manufacturing research and also profoundly influence the education of engineers in U.S. universities. Twenty centers have been selected so far.

ERCs are designed to establish a foundation of multidisciplinary, university-based engineering research. The government is to identify promising new fields of research and make grants to universities, which furnish matching funds and solicit contributions from corporations. Ultimately, universities and corporations take full responsibility for the centers.

Thus, ERCs are a direct attack on both the talent problem and the problem of engineering research. Because both universities and corporations are involved, the benefits flow both ways. Academic researchers gain the perspective of working on problems of economic importance and obtain access to research equipment that few universities can provide. Industry, in turn, gains access to the most creative minds among faculty members and graduate students. Here are some examples of what these Engineering Research Centers are undertaking:

At the Systems Research Centers at the University of Maryland, one of the first engineering centers designated, researchers have been working on computer software that will analyze weaknesses in factory production systems and design of a robotic arm that may one day be used in an orbiting space station.

The Center for Robotics Systems in Microelectronics at the University of California Santa Barbara is working with twenty companies, including Bell Communications Research, GM, IBM, Intel, and Plesscor.

The Advanced Combustion Engineering Research Center, a

joint effort of Brigham Young University and the University of Utah, is working on the use of low-cost fossil energy resources. The Netshape Manufacturing Center at Ohio State University seeks to develop processes that will manufacture a part near "netshape," eliminating the need for cutting or pressing out parts and thereby minimizing scrap. It is being joined by eighteen private companies.

Ten years ago, university-industry partnership to this extent was unimaginable. At that time, only a few universities had links to manufacturing that would provide their students with the background needed for today's changing manufacturing environment. Furthermore, any laboratory projects within universities were merely machine-shop practices, machining, or industrial engineering—good, pragmatic work for students, but not geared toward America's future needs.

As Nam Suh put it recently, institutions such as the ERCs are needed today "to nurture new ideas, encourage innovation, produce better educated people, and promote strong interaction among our institutions." The fact that we have begun to recognize the need for such interaction is a hopeful sign that cross-institutional partnerships will play an important role in the revival of U.S. manufacturing.

8

Human Resources

It is somewhat ironic—but perhaps typically Japanese—that the leading guardian of manufacturing quality in all of Japan is tucked inconspicuously into a remote and modest section of Tokyo that is almost impossible to find. The route to the offices of the Union of Japanese Scientists and Engineers is such a circuitous journey through twisting, winding, one-lane streets that even experienced taxi drivers must stop several times and ask postal carriers and police officers for directions.

I made this journey not long ago to talk with Juni Noguchi, the Union's executive director, about Japan's most prestigious award to industry—the Deming Prize. This prize, which is awarded each year by the Union, is sought aggressively by every Japanese company because it recognizes an attribute considered today to be quintessentially Japanese—industrial quality. Ironically, it is named for an American, Dr. W. Edwards Deming, the noted proponent of industrial quality who found a receptive audience in Japan after being all but ignored in the United States.

My purpose in visiting the Union of Japanese Scientists and Engineers was to learn how Emhart's companies in Japan might be considered as candidates for the Deming award, which I felt would be quite a coup for an American company to win. But Noguchi-san obviously felt differently. After listening to me, he spoke at great length through an interpreter. Although I do not understand Japanese, I could tell that he was lecturing me in a determined, stern tone of voice.

This came as a great surprise, because I know from experience that most Japanese business executives are reserved and tactful, at least at a first meeting. But Noguchi-san told me in no uncertain terms that an American company would have great difficulty winning the Deming Prize.

He acknowledged that some U.S. companies have won— IBM, for example. Generally speaking, though, U.S. companies are eliminated in the early stages of consideration. They generally get high marks for technology, he told me, but fail on the people side of the equation. "When U.S. companies supply us with their factory procedures," he said, "they lack programs that establish the environment for total company involvement in quality." He concluded by suggesting, "Mr. Rydz, perhaps you are reaching for an unachievable objective."

I am sure many of you will think that the Union of Japanese Scientists is merely trying to block U.S. companies from winning the Deming Prize—and, in fact, that thought occurred to me during my meeting with Noguchi-san. As I thought about it, however, I decided the truth was that Americans may not truly understand what Noguchi-san meant when he referred to quality.

When U.S. companies talk about Japanese quality, they think the Japanese are committed to *product* quality. But this is not what Noguchi-san meant. "Quality of products is important," he told me. "But it is not the major thrust of the requirements for winning the Deming Prize." In Japan, the quality of the product is not a goal in itself. It is the result of a total commitment on the part of the *employees* to do everything well. But I was not certain U.S. companies would ever understand Noguchi-san's concept of a total commitment to quality.

On the flight back from Japan, I began to reflect on my experience with Noguchi-san. It was then that I realized that we could not achieve quality in our products—or even in our overall commitment—simply by copying the Japanese. The secrets of their success lie deep in their own history and culture. Concepts such as quality circles work for them because they grow out of Japan's cultural heritage. We cannot hope to copy Japan's success in business simply by superimposing their techniques on our work force.

Instead, we must forge a new generation of success in manufacturing by building on our own strengths and our own culture, just as the Japanese have. Along the way, we can certainly learn from other nations. But ultimately we must compete with the Japanese (and other foreign manufacturing powers) as Americans, not as pseudo-Japanese.

The Importance of the Work Force

Throughout this book, I have emphasized the need to *rethink* the nature of manufacturing—to challenge accepted traditions of how things are done in order to meet the all-new problems and opportunities we face today. I have frequently laid the blame for manufacturing's problems at the feet of plant managers and their corporate bosses, whom I believe to be tied to the past. A major reason I have written this book is to awaken these two groups of leaders to new opportunities. But even if managers and executives change their thinking, it would make little difference unless the people who work for them are willing to take up the challenge as well.

In order for us to compete effectively, we must remember the workers themselves are of primary importance. Whatever technological advances are introduced, people will use that technology. Whatever changes financial experts might make in capital budgeting, people will specify and use the equipment purchased with that capital. The common denominator in all the forces of change discussed in this book is that *people who work for the company* must take responsibility for making change happen.

Management mavens—including myself—can talk all they want about things like product quality and lower costs. But after my conversation with Noguchi-san, I realized that these are not really goals in themselves. They are the end-product of an environment that fosters good work by all employees. If we copy anything about the Japanese, we should copy their understanding that this is true. If U.S. companies want people to take maximum advantage of the opportunities presented by change, then they must change their policies relating to those people.

I believe this change must come about in two steps. First, we must understand that the nature of factory work is changing dramatically. Manual skill is being replaced by brainpower even on the shop floor. Thus, we must recognize that the changing nature of factory work means that we probably have to rethink the way we design jobs, job classifications, and human resource policies.

The second step, I believe, is to use this opportunity to build on the natural strengths of the American worker. In recent years, the American factory worker has gained a reputation as unproductive and overpaid—the primary reason the United States loses manufacturing jobs to other nations. As I hope the previous chapters in this book have shown, labor cost is not always as important a factor in plant relocation as we might suspect. Likewise, American workers are not lazy and overpaid. Quite the contrary, they are often highly motivated and far more skilled than their foreign counterparts at adapting to rapidly changing situations. In reconstructing the way our factory jobs are organized, we must take maximum advantage of the opportunity presented to us in the form of the American worker.

In this chapter I don't intend to focus on the role of the human resources or personnel department and how that role ought to change because I am less concerned with the bureaucracy of the work force than with the work force itself. Motivating Americans to produce quality work is the relevant consideration here; understanding job classifications and personnel forms isn't. The human resources bureaucracy within every corporation will no doubt remain and will continue to perform the important tasks of hiring and monitoring the work force. But managers throughout the factory must understand and internalize new approaches to dealing with that work force.

The Changing Nature of Factory Work

To understand how deeply embedded the traditional factory has become in our human resources (and union) structures, simply think about all the industrial job classifications so familiar to us—shop-floor laborer, paint sprayer, polisher, drafting-room supervisor, stenographer, time-card clerk, bookkeeper, shop-floor stock chaser, drawing checker, time-study engineer, director of personnel. All reflect the structure of traditional U.S. factories as laid out by Frederick Winslow Taylor: Burgeoning labor classifications, dedicated mechanical skills, and operators restricted to specific machines represent a segmented collection of crafts, specific skill levels, and restricted job duties.

Now think about the kind of factory these job titles imply. Jobs such as expediters, checkers, and chasers were established because factories could not do things right the first time. Bookkeepers and time-card checkers functioned as scorekeepers, but all too often, as we have seen, they keep score of the wrong things over the wrong time period. And traditional human resources people—under the guise of personnel or industrial relations department—spend their time tracking the number of grievances and absenteeism trends.

These jobs have little to do with giving employees the opportunity to grow, explore, contribute; they only limit them from doing certain things. And in the traditional factory, this made a great deal of sense. As Taylor, the father of industrial job classification, pointed out, the traditional factory relied on its blue-collar workers *not* to think but to perform mechanical tasks by rote.

These tasks sometimes required skill and sometimes strength, but they did not require creativity. As I have said before in this book, the traditional factory was designed to standardize the work required of human employees—or, as public opinion researchers Daniel Yankelovich and John Immerwahr put it, to ensure that "high productivity required only a limited commitment from the workforce." In short, the factory could be kept humming even if the workers were not motivated.

Things are different now. The jobs requiring muscle and rote—even those that require some skill, such as machining—are being automated. The production of a huge volume of standardized units isn't as important as it once was. Because of sophisticated technologies, activities on the shop floor are more interdependent. Within each unit, fewer employees are responsible for a particular task, meaning every employee has more responsibility. Slight machine malfunctions can throw an entire line off a carefully orchestrated production schedule and cost a great deal of money, and so they must be corrected immediately.

That means even shop-floor jobs in the future will require a great deal of diagnostic and analytical skill. Workers must be willing to share information and participate in problem solving with their supervisors. As manufacturing technology becomes more advanced and integrated, each worker must be more knowledgeable and more willing to assume an active role, not simply a passive role, in the factory's operations. These are the people who keep today's factory humming—but if they aren't motivated to do their jobs well, the factory *won't* hum.

For these new employees to do the best they can, they should not be approached by management as an unfortunate cost that must be held back through rigid job classifications and personnel regulations. Rather, they must be viewed truly as human *resources* and given an environment in which they can identify and take advantage of the opportunities presented in technology, finance, global competition, and external relationships.

Unfortunately, manufacturing managers rarely approach human resource issues with this view in mind. Their minds are geared toward machines, not people. They may do extensive studies and analyses about new products and new processes, but they'll rarely consider how these advances will affect the work force or vice versa. Some plant managers will plop an automated machine down on the factory floor without thinking about how to redesign the manufacturing process to make the machine more useful. Likewise, some plant managers will bring new machines into the workplace without thinking about how the work force and job classifications can be rearranged to take advantage of all new opportunities the machine presents. They can wind up with a factory that purchases a flexible manufacturing system but still has stock chasers on the payroll.

To a certain extent, some changes in human resources will be forced on our manufacturing companies by competitive conditions. New technology will alter, and in some cases eliminate, manufacturing jobs. Financial pressures and worldwide pressures will redistribute corporate resources across the globe; that, too, will affect jobs and working conditions. And the growing need for external relationships—with governments, universities, even competitors—will require many employees to become more innovative and more broadly focused.

But simply reacting to these changes will not bring out the best in our employees. In fact, given our recent history, a reactive posture might create nothing but more trouble. Our human resources policies have to equip these workers to adapt to change and make maximum use of the opportunities it represents. Traditional human resources policies didn't—and still don't.

Redesigning Jobs

The single most important tool in overhauling a factory's human resources is *the redesigning of jobs* to fit both the modern factory and the American personality. Even as automation has taken away many low-skill jobs, U.S. managers have sought to deskill the jobs that remain so the factory can still operate with minimal commitment from the workers. But redesigning jobs—creating more challenging positions, broadening worker skills, allowing each employee to become more versatile, and so forth—can help create an environment in which American workers can flourish.

Let me use the presence of flexible manufacturing systems in the factory as an example. As I have stated several times in this book, one of the keys to the revival of U.S. manufacturing is the use of such systems. They allow factories to manufacture custom products or produce items in small quantities just as quickly and inexpensively as they would produce a large run of one product. But U.S. companies have not used flexible manufacturing to maximum advantage. Why? One reason is the traditional, rigid system of job classifications left over from an earlier era.

Often, this resistance to change has held back not just the company but also the workers and the unions as well. Factory workers who handle one machine each, for example, may have a great deal of idle time once much of their activities have been automated. As their numbers dwindle and their idle time grows, the influence of their union over the factory's practices—and over the workers' welfare—declines.

But providing workers with multiple skills can help eliminate this problem. There is strong evidence that the companies that are willing to move away from traditional job classifications and broaden their workers' skills are gaining a competitive edge. And evidence also suggests that unions that assist in this effort also assist in maintaining their own influence and preventing manufacturing jobs from leaving the country.

For example, the Manufacturing Studies Board recently

conducted a survey of several companies that broadened their human resources policies. These companies included Cummins Engine, Ford, General Motors, IBM, and Mc-Donnell Douglas. The survey found that enormous changes are occurring in the field. For example, one unionized automobile components plant with a $60 million flexible manufacturing system has only three hourly job classifications. A unionized aerospace plant has reduced its job classifications from twenty to five. The reduction of job classifications was almost always accompanied by a broadening in the scope of activities for each classification.

As the Manufacturing Studies Board points out, broadening the scope of work can reduce overhead costs in two ways: Line workers can take over some jobs from support personnel, and jobs can be combined. In each case, worker and machine down time is minimized, labor resources are used more efficiently, and the factory becomes more productive and less costly to operate. The productive use of worker and machine down time has become, in effect, a strategic advantage for a U.S. factory.

In factories where this sort of job reform has occurred, the results have been dramatic. And they need not be traumatic. At one of its automotive paint plants, Sherwin-Williams encouraged broad employee job knowledge by paying a wage increment for each new skill learned. The results: A year after this program was launched, more than 95 percent of the work force had developed new skills. Within two and one-half years, product quality had improved and labor costs were cut in half.

The Manufacturing Studies Board found similar results at one of the plants it used as a case study. In a plant with 2,100 employees, the plant manager reduced the number of inspectors by fifty over a two-year period by giving the machine operators more responsibility for quality. No inspectors were laid off because the move was implemented during a period of growth, making it easier to use ordinary attrition to reduce the staff. (Not only was the staff made more efficient, but giving the operators more responsibility improved quality *and* lowered the cost of manufacturing.)

If union, employees, and management work together, automation can often mean greater profitability for the company and greater security for the workers. In many cases, this means involving the shop-floor workers and the unions in helping to automate the factory from the beginning. At some unionized factories, plant managers have asked workers and union reps to help select and organize the automated equipment to be purchased. In other cases, workers have been assigned to the development lab to work with manufacturing engineers on designing new equipment. In many cases, the result is a more efficient manufacturing operation—because the people who know the shop floor best are involved.

In Milwaukee the Allen Bradley Company, which manufactures automation control hardware, combined a new flexible manufacturing system and a more flexible work force, with the union's consent, to produce a much more efficient factory. As was discussed in Chapter 5, many U.S. companies have not used flexible manufacturing systems well. In many cases, they merely turn out a limited number of parts as an extension of traditional assembly-line manufacturing. But the Allen Bradley system can quickly adapt to customer demand for new products. In fact, though the system was set up to handle only 124 different product versions, it now produces 770 versions. The 45,000-square-foot system can produce 600 units per hour with only six attendants overseeing the shop floor.

Allen Bradley executives say they have dramatically broadened the scope of their flexible manufacturing system by identifying new customers who require different configurations. But they wouldn't have been able to do that without the assistance of the union and the workers themselves. Because the union relaxed its work rules, the company was able to set up the flexible manufacturing process without being confined by them. And Allen Bradley executives also say the employees assigned to the project were involved from the beginning, forming an emotional attachment to the project.

If the union had fought the flexible system or required traditional work rules, the workers would have been hardest hit—because automation would have meant fewer jobs to produce the same number of units. But by mutually agreeing to shed outmoded employee policies, the company, the union, and the workers themselves were able to vastly expand the company's potential for sales, as well as the need for production workers knowledgeable in automated machinery. By rethinking and redesigning job classifications, the factory was able to remain competitive and many workers were able to keep their jobs.

Tapping the Strengths of the American Work Force

Though redesigning jobs is important, it alone cannot bring out the full potential of the work force. Our human resources policies must be built on techniques and approaches derived from our own cultural background. Within American culture lie several characteristics that can be tapped effectively in this effort: a strong sense of individual pride, the desire on the part of American workers to know they are doing something important, and a combination of the first two—American-style teamwork. Though they're usually highly individual, American workers love challenge and competition, and they'll work together on teams to prove they're the best—especially when an important goal is on the line.

These characteristics can play an important role in making a manufacturing operation competitive today. Workers need to be able to work independently as individuals. But they also must work together toward strategic goals. Let's look at each of these items in more detail.

Individual Pride

The most important characteristic—and the one most different from the Japanese—is the strong sense of individuality that runs through American culture. Americans see themselves as individuals. This does not mean they cannot work in teams or as part of large organizations. But it does mean they place a high priority on *individual recognition* for their work. Even in the traditional, brawn-over-brains American factory, the machine operator had a great deal of pride in his own work.

As responsibility is decentralized on the shop floor, pride becomes an important element in the success of a plant. In a sense, pride becomes a strategic tool in manufacturing because the plant's ability to implement changes and adapt to different conditions depends, in large part, on workers' initiative. But as American factories come under greater attack from worldwide competitors, American workers often have been accused of a lack of pride. If American workers were proud of their work, critics say, we would not lose out to Japan and other countries, particularly in the competition for high-quality products.

I don't believe that American workers lack pride. However, I do believe that the traditional American factory discouraged them from taking pride in their work. In many cases, emphasis on pride has been replaced with emphasis on job security and pension benefits, which to a certain extent made sense in the factory that required workers to conduct repetitive, low-skill tasks. After all, who could maintain active pride in a job designed to reduce one's work to the lowest common denominator? Other motivators were required.

But is pride dead in American workers or simply dormant? There is ample evidence that pride plays an important role in the underlying values of American workers. For instance, a report by the Aspen Institute found that 52 percent of American workers endorse "a strong form of work ethic," as opposed to 26 percent in Germany and only 17 percent in Britain. Public opinion researchers Daniel Yankelovich and John Immerwahr found similar results. Only 22 percent of American workers they surveyed said they were performing to their full capacities, and 44 percent said they did not put much into their work beyond what was required. But 52 percent agreed they had "an inner need to do the very best job I can, regardless of pay," and two-thirds said they prefer a boss who demands high-quality workmanship.

Thus, I believe pride is present—if dormant—in the American worker. Clearly, redesigning jobs to give individual workers more responsibility is the first step toward tapping the reservoir of pride. In fact, maybe the best way to instill pride in the shop floor today is to recognize outstanding workers with analytical and diagnostic skills by giving them a separate career path. At present, the only promotion available on most shop floors is to the job of foreman. But the most outstanding workers are not always the best foremen, especially if workers rely on brainpower rather than relations with fellow workers to get the job done.

Under the separate-path concept, workers with interpersonal skills could still be promoted to foreman; workers equally proficient in analytical and diagnostic skills could be promoted along a separate path, with equal pay and prestige within the company. In fact, some of our largest companies have already adopted aspects of this idea in the research area. Eastman Kodak has created the position of senior research associate for research engineers who have technical expertise but are not well suited for managerial positions. AT&T, similarly, has created the position of senior scientist. But this idea should not be limited to the research lab. It would be just as valuable on the shop floor, giving title, pay, and prestige equivalent to a foreman's job to a senior machinist who makes an extraordinary contribution to the operation.

But perhaps the most important way to tap pride is simply to communicate the company's goals and reinforce each worker's sense of importance. American companies generally do a poor job of communicating a company's strategy. In particular, top management doesn't explain to the company the role of the manufacturing operation—and its people—in meeting that strategy.

But when a plant's management does undertake to communicate its ideas, workers respond. In the Manufacturing Studies Board's analysis of sixteen plants, the board found one unionized assembly plant in the Midwest that had developed a statement of philosophy that reinforced the management's goals and still gave workers a sense of pride. The statement said the plant's goal was "to provide an environment for employee involvement, an atmosphere of trust, of mutual respect and human dignity so that we may achieve our common goals of high quality, mutual success, job security, and effective community relationships." This was the plant that reduced job classifications from 200 to 34—and the plant managers traced that and many other innovative ideas for shop-floor success to that statement of philosophy.

The more individual recognition workers receive, the more pride they will have in their own work. The more these workers understand about the company's objectives, the harder they will work to achieve those objectives. The more the workers feel they are playing a team that is trying to win, the better they will play.

Focusing Innovative Effort

The second important characteristic of Americans is they want to know they are working on something important. If they recognize something as being of critical importance, they will respond to it—witness the tremendous success of telethons, which raise money to combat diseases. If Americans do not believe in the importance of an issue, they soon lose interest in it.

The same is true in the factory. If a research project or product line is not considered important by the company, those working on it will tend to lose pride and interest. If, on the other hand, the company has identified a particular issue as being of major importance, everyone in the company will respond and work extra hard to bring the project to fruition.

This is also true among foreign workers, of course. But Japanese workers, for example, have responded more to the nationalistic idea that whatever their manufacturing job entails—no matter how obscure it might seem within the corporate structure—it is important for the country that they do it well. American workers, by contrast, are motivated by importance within the factory setting. They will respond to a focused demand for excellence.

When I worked at the Singer's plant in Elizabeth, New Jersey, we held a monthly factory management meeting to prepare the "ten most wanted" list. But we weren't after criminals. We were after the ten highest-priority problems in the factory. Managers brought their candidates, and by consensus we agreed on ten critical areas that then were communicated to all personnel throughout the factory. A key milestone chart was reviewed in order to ensure that progress was being made on each one. When one item was removed from the list, another took its place. In short, the "ten most wanted" list was a focused attempt to bring innovative opportunities to the attention of everyone in the factory, so those problems could be solved.

Innovation is clearly a top priority in any manufacturing organization today. But how to instill an innovative spirit in the work force is a tough question. Many experts on innovation suggest that it is best fostered by letting employees loose—giving them a great deal of freedom and little discipline. In fact, there is a widespread belief in our culture that a free-flowing environment somehow releases people to think more freely and innovatively.

But I don't believe this is true—at least not for American workers. Throughout my manufacturing experience, I have encountered many instances of innovation at all levels. Yet

I have rarely seen these innovations arise out of an unstructured, undisciplined environment. Instead, they usually grew out of a specific challenge issued by management, such as those identified on our "ten most wanted" lists. As management guru Peter Drucker put it recently in the Spring 1985 *Harvard Business Review* article, "The Discipline of Innovation," "Most innovations, . . . especially successful ones, result from a conscious, purposeful search for innovating opportunities which are found only in a few situations."

I couldn't agree more. I believe American workers respond not to some amorphous pledge of freedom but to a focused challenge to improve something that needs to be improved.

As my story about the "ten most wanted" list suggests, the key to this kind of innovating, as with pride, is communication within the company. You shouldn't issue a challenge unless you are sure that the work force hears you. This requires a sustained effort on the part of managers to communicate the challenge, round up the ideas, champion the good ones, and explain why others are rejected. Otherwise, even if it began with the best intentions, a factory-wide search for innovation will end not with success but with a common complaint from the shop floor: "They're not listening, so the heck with it."

In 1984 Emhart decided to combat the "heck with it" attitude by establishing an annual Technology Innovation Award. The award is presented every year to a select group from Emhart's operating units for outstanding technical innovations. It consists of three elements: The first is cash; the second is an attractive trophy, created especially for this award by Don Genaro, senior partner with Henry Dreyfuss Associates, an internationally known industrial design firm; third—and maybe most important—is recognition.

For starters, the final selection is made not by the corporate staff but by the technology committee of Emhart's board of directors. The award is presented personally by

Peter Scott, Emhart's chairman and chief executive officer, at a meeting of the board of directors. Also in attendance are the Emhart group presidents with whom the innovators were associated.

The message is inescapably clear: Technological innovation is a high priority at Emhart, and at the highest levels the corporation will recognize not only the innovators themselves but the executives who foster innovation. Since 1984 there have been 105 submissions, accounting for well over $200 million in new product sales, as well as $50 million in cost savings because of innovation in manufacturing processes.

And we have no intention of discontinuing the program. The more established our recognition program becomes, the harder it will be for anybody in our organization to say, "They're not listening, so what the heck." No matter who they are or what they do at Emhart, they'll be challenged and motivated to work on innovations. That's good for the company and for the workers themselves.

Teamwork

As I said before, Americans are not so individual that they won't work in teams. But teamwork must be carefully structured to accentuate the strengths of the American workers. Americans won't work in teams simply because they are assigned to them; but they *will* work in teams when they have a goal to achieve and when a sense of competition gets their blood pumping.

A few years ago, the quality circle was advertised as a leading reason for Japanese manufacturing success and was imported to the United States as the latest management panacea. Quality circles were small teams of workers who made up a self-contained unit, supposedly inspiring each other to greater creativity and better work. Quality circles are alive and well in Japan, but in 1986 *Fortune* magazine—calling them

"Hula-Hoops of 1980's management"—reported that they were in trouble here in the United States.

In a way, this is not surprising. The overall concept—giving a group of workers more independence and more responsibility for their work—makes sense. In fact, it meshes nicely with the idea that American workers have a large reservoir of untapped pride. But the quality circle is another example of a Japanese method that works well in Japan but not here. The quality circle succeeds in part because Japanese workers are thirsty for social experiences outside their homes after hours, and so quality circles are transformed into a social experience.

American workers have no such thirst because we have more than enough opportunities for socializing outside work already. But that does not mean the concept of self-reliant teamwork cannot succeed in the American factory. It *can* succeed—when the team is given a cause.

A few years ago, I oversaw the creation of a just-in-time inventory program at Emhart's True-Temper hardware plant in Anderson, South Carolina. Just-in-time is another Japanese-created panacea to manufacturing problems, but it has proven helpful if used correctly.

The objective of the just-in-time program is to set up smoother and less complicated production flows and also to reduce inventory to rock-bottom levels. At True-Temper management selected a team, made up of both hourly workers and supervisors, to face the challenge of a more effective production control system. The team came up with a solution called the production pull system, which limits the amount of inventory actually on hand in the factory. Work in process has been reduced by 28 percent because the members of the team recognized that they were part of something important and rose to the occasion.

Why are quality circles a flop in the United States, while other teamwork efforts, such as the just-in-time inventory program at True-Temper, succeed? At True-Temper we were building on the American workers' strongest attributes. We didn't want to give them a substitute for their bowling league; we wanted to take their desire to be the best and place it in a highly structured situation, so they could solve a problem. And it succeeded. The group worked very hard, with each member testing another's creativity to get to the root of the problem and solve it.

Throughout these last five chapters, I have discussed a wide variety of concerns—technology, global forces, finance, external relationships, and human resources. But I hope that in each chapter, the same message has come across. To remain competitive in the face of galloping technological change and a fast-paced worldwide competition, we must change the way we think about manufacturing. We cannot assume that our standard way of doing business—whether it's allocating product cost or designing job classifications— will serve us well in the future. We must continue to find new ways to make our factories, and our workers, more efficient and more productive—by searching for hidden opportunities in the factory (such as the flexibility of the American worker) and using them to their maximum possible advantage.

Part IV

Bringing It All Together

9

Can We Make What Went Wrong Go Right?

Robotics, computer-aided design, computer-aided manufacturing, computer-integrated manufacturing, flexible manufacturing systems—these technological concepts are familiar to us all. Each has been touted as a panacea for U.S. manufacturing ills. And if these technological cure-alls aren't enough, add these—quality of work life, quality circles, theory X, theory Y, just-in-time, also all being touted as solutions to industry's ills.

Indeed, these all are important. In fact, they always have been important because many of these concepts, technical and nontechnical, are fundamental to the survival and growth of a manufacturing operation. However, it is time to review what has gone wrong with U.S. manufacturing and see why these approaches have not achieved the anticipated levels of performance improvement.

What Went Wrong

What has gone wrong? Over a decade ago, the factory of the future was everyone's vision. Product designs spewing from CAD systems would connect directly to machines on the shop floor. Robots would replace menial repetitive work. Within minutes, it was predicted, production lines could switch from making electric toasters to room heaters. According to the experts, productivity would increase, quality would soar, and product costs would plummet.

What went wrong? It didn't quite happen the way that proponents of these panaceas predicted. Granted, there have been advances. Today as I visit our factories, there is robotic paint spraying equipment operating in places where humans should not be. Robots are loading and unloading hot metal in die casting operations. There are islands of automation in operations where a decade ago traditional manual assembly was the predominant way to produce many products. But like many who are fostering and encouraging major changes in the factory, I am not seeing the significant improvements that should be occurring. What went wrong?

When I joined Emhart in 1980, I had an excellent opportunity to see firsthand what was taking place in the early years of this decade using the technologies that promised so much for the factory of the future. Prior to my appointment as the vice president of technology for Emhart, I spent two years as Emhart's corporate director of productivity, a new position that allowed me to become fully acquainted with the corporation's vast global operation.

What I learned was a continuation of my experiences at the Singer Company, where as the vice president and chief technical officer for the Sewing Products Group I also had the opportunity to help implement programs for improving Singer's vast worldwide engineering and manufacturing organization.

At both Singer and Emhart I achieved a better understanding of why the factory of the future promises did not materialize as predicted. Let me share some of those observations:

1. The change of culture needed to upgrade a factory was, and still is today, misunderstood, underestimated, and often missing in company strategies and plans.

2. Infrastructure changes are not always implemented in the factory or in the company before bringing in advanced technology.

Let me address the first of these major issues, quality, in this chapter and infrastructure in the next.

Understanding the Culture

Even though many companies are now designing products for manufacturing, putting in place optimum shop-floor layouts and using the most advanced technology, the factory of the future can be defeated by a company's overall culture, divisional subcultures, and many subdivisions of these subcultures existing on the shop floor, in the front office, and even with top management.

Throughout a factory, cultures can make or break a factory manager. Cultures can defeat even the best of intentions, yet very little is understood about them. Perhaps the key to understanding factory cultures is to identify the critical cultures and which of these need to be changed or eliminated in order for change to occur. Based on my shop-floor experiences, two major cultures need to be understood:

1. In many factories today, quality is synonymous with an inspection culture. Quality control implies inspection, which fosters a culture of reject or accept, scrap or use. In many cases the factory operates through deviations from specifications. Inroads are being made in changing employee attitudes toward quality, but many companies continue to inspect for quality and have quality control infrastructure rather than the culture of quality assurance. "Make it right the first time" just has not been accepted in many companies—even today.

2. A second prevailing culture in many factories is the short-term attitude. The heroes on the shop floor are those who can keep production lines moving, solve problems, and meet

the day-by-day shipping requirements—in short, the fire-fighters. Certainly, there is a need for this type of activity; however, in most factories this short-term culture oversha-dows plans and strategies to correct underlying problems.

The Quality Inspection Culture

In the traditional view of quality, emphasis has been placed on determining a level of quality that is economically ac-ceptable to the company and then inspecting the product to make sure that nothing below that level gets shipped.

The Japanese, in contrast, build quality into their prod-ucts, their processes, and the way they operate. Many U.S. factories don't create quality from the beginning; they in-spect for it later. Unfortunately, inspecting quality is like applying a Band-Aid: It covers the wound but doesn't heal it.

Perhaps the best way to illustrate this culture difference is with an example. When I was vice president of engineer-ing at Singer, I was placed in charge of worldwide quality assurance for the Sewing Products Group. As part of my effort to improve quality, I decided to conduct a worldwide evaluation of Singer machines versus the competition. These tests also allowed us to rank Singer's twenty-six worldwide manufacturing plants in comparison with each other.

The results were startling. The United States finished eighth. Singer's German factory ranked first. And the Jap-anese factory finished second, even though the Japanese Singer factory had been manufacturing that particular ma-chine for less than two years—a remarkable achievement, in our opinion.

Naturally, on my next visit to Japan I praised the engi-neering and manufacturing departments for such a fine per-formance. I told them it was a great accomplishment that they had finished second among Singer's twenty-six world-wide factories. During the lunch period, Morakawa-san, the general manager of Singer's Japanese factory, asked to be excused from lunch to conduct a meeting with his personnel. I assumed that they wanted to determine how best to respond to our positive comments and our praise for a job well done in capturing second place.

After lunch, however, the general manager politely thanked me for the presentation that placed his plant second in the world of Singer factories in quality control. He then made the announcement that he and his management team had replaced the quality control manager during lunch with a new man who would report to the highest levels of the company. The Japanese were not satisfied to be number two on the list; they wanted to be number one. Interestingly, the general manager of the number eight factory (in the United States) exhibited no concern other than, ''Well, the Japanese do a better job.''

I don't ordinarily like to point to the Japanese and say that we should do things the way they do because I don't believe strengths that arise out of Japanese culture can be applied successfully in the American workplace. However, quality should be an exception. When the Japanese learned to concentrate on making products right in the first place, U.S. manufacturing was instantly at a disadvantage. When our companies tried to fight back, they did so without abandoning the culture of quality control, which put us at a further disadvantage. As with the industrial engineering culture, the entire manufacturing process had been arranged around the assumption that controlling quality, rather than creating it, was right. Conditions have changed, but the original assumptions have not been challenged nor changed.

Short-Term Culture

In the sixties financially oriented executives began to replace old-line manufacturing chiefs. They brought with them a new culture that ultimately worked against them—the short-term culture.

The short-term culture places the emphasis on quarterly profits over long-term stability. It's quite obviously connected to the financially oriented goals of the executives who rose to the tops of U.S. corporations in the sixties and seventies. This short-term culture grew and now pervades many factories today.

Factory firefighting is a culture that entices many managers and employees. However, this short-term culture is often fostered at the expense of long-term programs that seek to correct the cause of the problem. Those who have the vision and the ability to make long-term corrections are generally considered as overhead—and ultimately are often eliminated through cost reduction programs.

The culture within a factory often favors the problem solvers, but in too many situations the wrong problem is being worked on. Problem identifiers are actually more valuable in the factory since they accurately identify the problem.

A typical scenario confronting factory management is related to the short-term expectations of factories. A sales forecast is provided to a factory, either at the beginning of a calendar year or at some other point in time, such as the beginning of the month. Based on that forecast, factories attempt to plan their production workloads, materials purchases, delivery schedules, and resource requirements.

In general, just about every factory general manager that I speak with says that people start out with good intentions but in general do not adhere to the forecast throughout the time period for which it is intended. Deviations from the forecast can and do occur.

It should be pointed out that the short-term culture of a factory is generally the cause of situations that create problems. Factories operate on the basis that they are the bottleneck for achieving certain levels of revenue and profit performance. Throughout a factory, the last week of the month is a nightmare. Whatever it takes to ship the product occurs in just about every factory. When raw materials do not reach the factory on time, the entire schedule is upset. When a company attempts to buffer materials because of the danger that shipments might not reach production levels, inventories increase. This, of course, causes a problem relative to cash flow. A factory operating under these conditions is in a Catch-22 situation. If problems occur due to machine downtime and a factory manager builds inventory to compensate, the increase in inventory changes ratios negatively. On the other hand, if this step isn't taken, the sales organization is immediately at the doorstep deploring the possibility of lost revenues.

Throughout all this firefighting, it is very difficult for factory managers to have long-range plans that can anticipate the many problems that occur within the factory. Yet unless factory managers practice some long-range planning, long-range scheduled machine maintenance, and machine capability studies, the factory will continue to operate in a state of chaos in which short-term firefighters continue to keep things churning.

Those of us who have been on the factory floor realize how easy it is to be caught up in the short-term mentality that pervades a factory. Consider, for example, a case I was involved in at Singer Company relative to product lines that used powdered-metal oil-impregnated bushings to avoid the need to oil sewing machines.

Oil-less sewing machines required bushings that had oil-impregnated powdered metal. As shafts rotated within these bushings, they became lubricated by the oil that was contained within the bushings themselves. Hence, the machines could be advertised as ''never needing oiling.''

On one occasion, a batch of bushings arrived from the supplier that were not produced to specification. Thus, the machines that were being manufactured seized up or became noisy. It was soon discovered that the bushings were out of spec and did not meet the requirements of oil-less operation.

While machines were being rejected, frantic telephone

calls were made to the vendor only to learn that the next batch of bushings would not arrive for several weeks. Under these conditions the factory would have to be shut down, people sent home, and shipments not met. Unfortunately, this incident occurred prior to shipping for a Christmas season, which added to the woes of the factory manager; these kinds of problems seem to occur at the worst possible time. Whoever is "up there" doesn't always look after factory managers.

As the chief technical officer for the group, I was called to the shop floor by the factory manager to determine how best to keep the factory lines moving. One proposed solution was to remove the oil-impregnated bearings completely, revert to the old bushings, and use oil cans to lubricate the shafts. This is what was traditionally done for sewing machines for many years, and the factory manager felt that the problems encountered with oil-impregnated bearings were just too great to overcome. He recommended returning to the old designs. The alternate solution proposed by engineering was to shut down the line, visit the vendor to discover why the oil-impregnated process was not working properly, and take steps with the vendor to speed up shipments of good bearings.

The factory manager rejected engineering's proposal and suggested that we meet with top management of the company to referee the battle. He recommended returning to the old design rather than attempt to correct the new production problems. His argument was based on the fact that one week of production losses would occur and this meant not only loss of shipments but a loss of sales, loss of jobs, and so on.

When confronted with the alternatives, I considered backing down and agreeing with the factory manager about returning to the old solution of using oil cans to lubricate. I stayed with my position not to revert to the old design, however, and suggested trying to find out what was required to correct the problem.

That is indeed what we did. The vendor's shop discovered what the source of the problem was and was able to make corrections that subsequently met the shipment of bushings at a higher rate. By using overtime, the Singer factory in Elizabeth, New Jersey, just about made up for the loss that occurred during the week.

The point I am making here is that the pressures of the moment began to influence my thinking to the point that I nearly abandoned the long-term solution and grasped the more immediate solution, which was, "Let's use oil cans and keep the production lines moving." I'm glad that I didn't give in. Of course, many unsuspecting mothers sewing their daughters' wedding dresses or prom gowns also benefited from the decision: The oil can solution would have ruined many a dress.

Culture, whether it is a quality-control mentality or short-term mentality, will stand in the way of the best plans within a factory. What is the solution?

Changing cultures is not easy. Persistence and openness often help create modify cultures. In many cases, however, major changes in an organization or in the infrastructure of the company are needed. The next chapter discusses changing the infrastructure, certainly one step that can help change the culture. In many respects, university/industry partnerships can help create these infrastructure changes needed in industry. So let's start with the university/industry partnership—the first step in creating the infrastructure change needed in a company.

10

Putting It All Together: The Universities

Unless specific actions are undertaken by universities, industry, and national and state governments, manufacturing will not achieve the gains that can be expected. Everyone talks about it, everyone is determined that something needs to be done, everyone has programs underway, yet unless certain key steps are taken, talk will merely continue. Some programs will be implemented, but most companies will not make significant strides.

The previous chapters have identified areas where manufacturing is faltering and in some cases suggested possible courses of action. This chapter and the next identify corrective actions that need to be taken in order for companies to restore their manufacturing competitiveness. This chapter identifies specific steps that universities can take to help implement manufacturing programs that can move the United States toward a stronger, competitive economic position.

Manufacturing Centers: Education and Research Is the Key

University manufacturing centers are being set up throughout the United States. In fact, there seems to be a bandwagon effect as many universities establish manufacturing centers one after another.

These newly established manufacturing centers should consider the goals of Wesley L. Harris, dean of engineering at the University of Connecticut. Harris, the main force behind bringing together the teams necessary to put UCONN into a strong position for a manufacturing center, recognizes the weaknesses of many of the present manufacturing centers now proliferating throughout academia. "The bottom line," according to Harris, "will be the ability of universities to create the courses and the teachers who can train future manufacturing leaders for industry." This is the main problem facing many manufacturing centers at universities. All too often industry managers use these centers to conduct manufacturing projects. There is nothing wrong with this approach providing that the projects are research-oriented and have educational goals rather than merely a project orientation. An industry university partnership should have as its major objectives upgrading industry personnel, improving the university graduates who will ultimately join industry, and uplifting the level of research needed to move industry to the forefront through manufacturing technology.

As a member of the advisory boards of several manufacturing centers, I've noted that some industrial members judge a manufacturing center on its ability to accomplish certain specific manufacturing tasks at a lower cost and in less time than the company could accomplish, either within their own organization or through consulting firms. Too often industry uses a university manufacturing center as a job shop. When a company contributes financially to a university center, company representatives may feel that their funding entitles them to a share of projects that can be accomplished at the center. In some cases, these projects are either routine or at a level that provides very little new knowledge.

In a National Science Foundation symposium conducted in 1985 Roland W. Schmitt, former GE executive and now president of Rensselaer Polytechnic Institute, stated, "A bridge established between universities and industry should carry much more than money. As one university president put it, 'Don't just send us your money, send us your people who understand the critical problems. Just sending money is not enough.' " Schmitt continued:

> "The idea is not to create centers that are, in effect, job shops for industry. . . . The research at the center should be fundamental research in the area of engineering practice being taken on by industry and the university. Its aims are not building robots for factories, but generating new understanding of the fundamentals of robotic vision, touch and control. Not programming expert systems for use in diagnostics or repair, but generating new understanding of knowledge representation, search and logic programming techniques, heuristic analogies, and the other fundamentals of an artificial intelligence; not building biotechnology production facilities, but developing unit operation concepts for biological processes.

Education Must Be First

At Emhart we were the pioneers of the manufacturing engineering applications center at Worcester Polytechnical Institute. In the late seventies and early eighties, Walter Abel, Emhart's vice president of research and development and my predecessor, had the foresight to see that Emhart needed a flow of manufacturing talent in order to provide manufacturing leaders who could create changes within many of Emhart's production facilities. From his idea of working closely with WPI, Emhart and WPI established MEAC, a manufacturing engineering application center.

The initial objectives of the center were to conduct fundamental research on automation systems that would create significant improvements throughout Emhart's production facilities. Personnel from Emhart were assigned to work at WPI and actually moved their offices into the WPI center.

Mike Ford, Emhart's chairman, president, and chief executive officer, promoted the project by mentioning it in his speeches and ensuring that the MEAC center received a prominent position in Emhart's annual reports and quarterly statements to the stockholders. Additionally, the internal publication the *Emhart News*, distributed to employees and stockholders, carried articles about the successes of the divisions that conducted programs at WPI.

The WPI program was successful. Robotic systems and automation proliferated throughout Emhart's manufacturing divisions. Emhart made significant strides through the WPI MEAC program. As the program matured, however, the WPI center began to be used by certain Emhart divisions to conduct projects that they either did not have the talent or the time to do themselves. We discovered that some divisions were using WPI as a low-cost means to handle projects rather than to conduct fundamental manufacturing research and most important to upgrade its personnel. These divisions were using MEAC as a job shop.

The divisions that took advantage of the education and basic research objectives of MEAC succeeded in upgrading their operations, but divisions that considered WPI a location for conducting projects did not achieve the same success. Mike Ford, Emhart's chairman, saw that the major problem was that all divisions were not taking full advantage of the major objectives of the university—mainly its educational capabilities.

A directive was issued from corporate that the divisions must consider hiring a WPI graduate and bring that graduate into their manufacturing operations. Several of the divisions have been very successful in upgrading their talent, and in many cases WPI graduates have been a major force behind creating changes within the manufacturing operations.

The objective of a manufacturing center at a university is to fulfill the major role of the university—education. As Eric Block, director of the National Science Foundation stated in the NSF 1985 symposium, ''The objective of centers is not only the involvement of scientists and engineers from many disciplines, but to form building links with industry with an emphasis on improving the teaching and practice of engineering.''

Attracting Small Companies to Universities: Innovative Approaches Needed

Although education is a major objective for manufacturing centers established at universities, innovative solutions are needed to bring small companies into these industry-university relationships. For years I have attended advisory board meetings where participants discuss how to attract small companies to the university center. In general, most professors associated with the center assume that small companies do not join university manufacturing centers because of the financial cost. The centers therefore attempt to attract small companies by establishing fees that they believe are reasonable for smaller companies. Generally, the fees are based on company sales: Larger companies pay more to join the centers, and smaller companies pay correspondingly less.

What is missed by most university centers is that the smaller companies simply do not have the time or talent necessary to take full advantage of a university manufacturing center. The problem can best be summarized by Norbert Fowler, chairman of the Committee on the Proposal for the Evaluation of Manufacturing Centers for the director of National Engineering Laboratory, National Institute of Standards and Technology. In the study conducted by the National Research Council published in November 1988, Fowler states that

> We believe that smaller companies are among those that can benefit most from the introduction of advanced manufacturing technology. Unfortunately, many of these companies lack the awareness, sophistication and resources

necessary to apply new technology. The greatest need of such companies is education. Someone to teach them that technologies are available, applicable to their needs and cost effective in their plans. A major effort is required to make technology transferable to a variety of companies as well as actually to accomplish the technology transfer.

The subject of how best to bring small companies into a manufacturing center membership was often discussed at MIT's laboratory for manufacturing and productivity advisory board meetings. Under David Hart, director for MIT's laboratory, the center agreed to an idea now being tried in Connecticut with the University of Hartford. I believe that the concept is worthy of further exploration at other university manufacturing centers.

Basically, the University of Hartford becomes a member of MIT's laboratory for manufacturing and productivity. Under the terms of the membership, a representative from the University of Hartford attends all center meetings and has access to the manufacturing capabilities at MIT. However, the University of Hartford membership is actually supported by fees from five small companies in the greater Hartford, Connecticut, area.

Through Murray Gerber, the chairman of the Connecticut Business and Industry Association, five small companies were selected to become affiliated with the University of Hartford. U of H in turn became a member of MIT's laboratory for manufacturing and productivity. Ray Christ, professor at University of Hartford, then became the liaison between the five smaller companies and MIT. He attends all meetings at MIT and reports the results to the five affiliates. Furthermore, as any of the five companies requires technical help, Ray Christ from the University of Hartford carries problems to MIT in order to help bring the technology at MIT back to the small company in Hartford.

This experiment taught us that small companies need more than funds to associate with large universities; they need personnel who are available to spend time at a center

such as MIT and have the technical sophistication to discover
where MIT can be helpful. By using a contact professor from
the University of Hartford as the representative for a group
of small companies, the member companies gain advantages
that come from being part of the MIT scene.

Using a local institution to represent a group of small
companies at a center at another university is a way by which
small companies can gain in many ways: They become
closely associated with a nearby university; they learn about
what is happening at other major universities where centers
are located; and they gain from the technology that is trans-
ferred from the center to the university. Through the local
universities, problems of the small company can be brought
to the attention of the large center and vice versa. In addition, personnel from both industry and the universities who
are members of the centers are aware of problems encountered by small companies. The education side of this program provides small companies the opportunity to upgrade
personnel, provides exposure for students, both at the local
university and the main center, and provides the means by
which both faculties can explore the problems encountered
by small companies, faculty members at local universities,
and faculty members at large centers.

11

Putting It All Together: Industry

Major changes must occur within universities, but changes also must occur within industry in order for manufacturing competitiveness to be restored. As Chapter 10 stated, the main objective of manufacturing centers in universities is to train and upgrade personnel. The major thrust needed within companies is total commitment. Unless there is total commitment to quality within a company, manufacturing will not restore competitiveness to U.S. companies.

Top Management Commitment Is Critical

Top executives must make long-term commitments to improve manufacturing. Managers must nurture the vision and plan the strategies that set the direction for manufacturing. All personnel must be ready to help implement these strategies. As a first step, top management must place manufacturing into the infrastructure of its strategic plan. Some companies have appointed vice presidents of technology, vice presidents of engineering, and vice presidents of manufacturing, but these executive officers are not effective unless they are part of the corporate strategy infrastructure. Unless they are in that strategic loop, these officers are merely functional heads directing operations rather than directing the future of their company. Unless manufacturing executives are also members of key operating committees within their company, they cannot be effective.

The Emhart Corporation under Mike Ford established an operating committee consisting of key executives. I was a member of that committee, so technology had representation at the highest level. Discussions pertaining to global strategies, new product strategies, and manufacturing involved all members of the operating committee. Hence, manufacturing was indeed part of the strategy loop at Emhart.

Boards of Directors Have a Role

An Emhart board of directors technology committee also was established. The board of directors technology committee was one of the major committees of Emhart's board of directors, and its major objective was to review the technology strategic plans of operating units and ensure that these strategies fit in with the overall corporate strategies and goals.

Through the board of directors technology committee, clear messages were sent throughout the company. Establishing the board committee sent a clear message throughout the divisions of the importance of technology. Furthermore, since manufacturing technology was considered a major thrust for the board committee reviews, various divisions were called in at regular intervals to review the status of their manufacturing programs and to present their strategies and vision of how they saw manufacturing fitting in to their overall plans.

Also, the board of directors and the corporate Office of Technology established an annual Emhart innovation award, given to the five or six outstanding innovations throughout Emhart's divisions. A significant number of these awards were related to innovations in manufacturing technologies that were being used by the divisions in the manufacturing operations and demonstrating clear performance achievements. Interest in the Emhart innovation award was extremely high, and all division presidents competed to win this award for their particular operating units.

What is key here is management commitment. Moreover, management commitment means money as well as time. Management must commit the time necessary to understand manufacturing and to understand the problems, strategies, and underlying principles that make up an effective manufacturing strategy.

Bringing Manufacturing into the Strategy Loop

All too often I have attended business reviews at which manufacturing is covered at the end of a meeting, generally when not much time is left. In many cases manufacturing's participation is merely a tour designed for everyone to "stretch their legs and walk around and see what's going on within the factory." In general, these types of meetings don't have the time for full discussions of manufacturing strategies.

Winning companies have manufacturing strategies. Consider the case of Xerox Corporation's manufacturing quality strategy. Through this strategy Xerox's manufacturing units reduced defects from 10,000 per million to 300 parts per million and is reducing these defects still further. Manufacturing costs in 1988 are half of the 1980 figure. Xerox copiers have regained market dominance, and several major competitors have since dropped out of the field.

In an April 17, 1989, *Industry Week* article, David Kearns, CEO of Xerox, discusses his strategy. He states that the first time he heard the term total quality control, he did not understand it. At first he thought it referred to quality control as learned in school and part of the traditional culture of manufacturing. After studying the process with Japanese associates at Fuji Xerox, he learned that TQC means how a business is run—in its entirety. It has nothing to do with checking quality as products roll off the assembly line. Kearns was driven to a quality focus as the need for change at Xerox grew out of two factors—competition and customer requirements. Xerox had not had any competition for a long period of time; its manufacturing costs were way too high, overhead was too large, and it was a very complicated organization. There also was a real lack of understanding about what Xerox customers really wanted. Kearns undertook a total change in Xerox's strategy, with significant improvements.

According to the May 1989 *Management Review*, Kodak is another company that changed its entire culture by establishing a line-of-business structure where each business is accountable for worldwide research development and manufacturing. As noted in the article, better-defined product specifications were implemented at Kodak based primarily on anticipation of customer needs. Coming up with correct specifications is a difficult process that involves turning marketing intelligence into tangible numbers. However, it is a vital step. Following the lead of Toyota Motor Corporation of Japan—famous for sending engineers into the marketplace to listen to customers' murmurs and then translating their findings into new designs—Kodak formalized methods of collecting and evaluating customer comments and translated them into product specifications. Kodak also defines the process of product development more clearly. Their group has a formalized process with well-defined steps and checkpoints to lead Kodak through the product development process. They call the system the manufacturability assurance process or MAP. Kodak also uses a project management approach that involves representatives from manufacturing on the project team at the beginning. A project leader steers the group toward defining goals. The team members and its leaders change as the product moves through each stage. Each new team incorporates at least some members of the original team for continuity.

Within Kodak's operations employees are encouraged to move around among different departments. Personnel movement brings fresh insights into divisions that have become too set in their ways.

At Kodak the turnaround time for experimentation has been accelerated. Individual divisions now schedule and use shared equipment and allow time for experimentation in manufacturing. This requires capital investments that often discourage other companies but that are eventually proven worthwhile. No time is wasted at Kodak. Idle machine time is used to train personnel as well as to conduct process experiments. Kodak also establishes pilot facilities that are small-scale versions of production equipment.

Pilot facilities possess the same characteristics as production equipment but are used to produce small quantities of new products. In the larger stages of product development, Kodak manufactures a small amount of the new product to test customer reaction and then makes necessary adjustments before manufacturing and delivering the product in quantity.

The design and development of dedicated pilot facilities is another area where Kodak invests time and money. This requires a management commitment both to quality and to quicker product development. No matter how fast you develop a product, if it's not well made, there is no gain. A small-scale facility has many advantages. You don't have to shut down production equipment to test new products. Also, since the pilot facilities closely emulate production equipment, successful small-scale production ensures the manufacturability of the product in quantity.

Granted, the Kodak processes are primarily chemical in nature, and these types of manufacturing process lend themselves to pilot plant operations. It is my belief, however, that all manufacturing can benefit from setting up pilot plant operations in manufacturing before going into full-scale operations. A case in point is Tucker Fasteners in Birmingham, England, where engineers have developed dramatically new manufacturing techniques for the production of pop rivets. Before full-scale production began, several units were installed in a dedicated building and a pilot plant operation set up to debug these new automation systems.

Examples of Manufacturing Strategies

It might be instructive to review a few companies' manufacturing strategies to convey how manufacturing strategy can fit into the overall strategy of a business. A manufacturing strategy that ultimately led to the change in the business direction of a particular company was devised by Emhart's Glass Machinery Group. Over time this machinery group continued to build up its spare parts business. In most cases companies traditionally handle spare parts by manufacturing additional parts in each job lot, but the problem with this is the build up of inventory. Also, as so often happens, the parts that are in inventory are not always the parts that are required by the customer.

Emhart's Glass Machinery Group has taken a new approach to looking at its spare parts business. Its spare parts are now seen as a total business rather than merely a side line to producing its main product. Not only does the Hartford group set up its spare parts business as a separate entity, but it conducts research and development on these parts so that when a customer requests a spare part or a retrofit of a machine, Emhart's Glass Machinery Group is able to upgrade that customer through new technology with these new parts. Thus, Emhart's business now includes selling a complete retrofit of a machine with not only spare parts but innovative products that provide the customer with productivity improvements for their machines over the machine as it was originally purchased.

Singer's needle business is another example of where manufacturing technology enabled the company to not only improve its product but gain higher margins as well. The traditional process for making needles was a conventional die press process that produced needles requiring a considerable amount of polishing of the eye in order to achieve the degree of smoothness needed within the eye of the needle. Singer strategy was to use the cold forming of needles, which is a totally different technique of manufacturing. However, the new process produced needles to a higher degree of smoothness and higher quality, resulting in fewer snags. As a result Singer was able to achieve greater margins for its needles—clearly an example of adding value through manufacturing.

As an example of how U.S. government agencies can have a major impact on helping to make manufacturing companies more competitive, consider the case of the Malcolm Baldrige National Quality Award. This award honors U.S. companies that achieve high levels of total quality management. Named after former Secretary of Commerce Malcolm Baldrige, the award was established by legislation—the Malcolm Baldrige National Quality Improvement Act of 1987, which was passed in August 1987.

The award is presented annually and is intended to help motivate U.S. companies, both large and small, to improve their total quality management, including the quality of their products and services. It was presented for the first time at a White House ceremony in November 1988.

I'd like to relate how this award affected one of Emhart's companies, Mallory Controls, which submitted an application for the award. Although Mallory was not one of the companies that received the award, attempting to win this award proved to be stimulating in itself.

Mallory Controls, with headquarters in Indianapolis, Indiana, makes electromechanical and electronic timers and controls for the appliance and automotive industries. Mallory is the leading supplier of appliance controls to companies such as Whirlpool and Maytag, and in 1988 it was honored as supplier of the year by a division of White Consolidated Industries, a major appliance maker.

Under the leadership of Mallory Controls former president Blake Humphrey and its present president Lowell Kilgus, Mallory has implemented successful automation programs, the primary objectives of which are to automate in order to improve product quality and reliability (see the discussion of their automation strategy in Chapter 3).

In 1988 Mallory controls entered the Malcolm Baldrige National Quality Award program sponsored by the U.S. Department of Commerce. Mallory's application was reviewed by three examiners from the Department of Commerce and one senior examiner, and the review was evaluated by three judges. All of this required approximately eighty hours expended in the examination of Mallory's application. As a result, an extensive report was received by Mallory from the Department of Commerce board of examiners identifying those areas that the board felt represented the strengths of Mallory and those that offered opportunities for improvement.

The report was positive in many respects, but Mallory was not a finalist. Lowell Kilgus, however, is using this report to rally the organization to once again go for the award after corrective action is taken to improve the areas that were pointed out by the board of examiners. Of course, Mallory Controls should consider its performance as exemplary since the final rating placed them beside many companies well known for their quality and realizability programs. Nevertheless, "winning is everything" and Mallory is going to aggressively pursue this award in the future. The board of examiners' report will serve as the basis for all employees to focus on areas where improvements are needed. In this regard the Malcolm Baldrige National Quality Award was indeed a very successful experience for Mallory.

The first three winners of the Baldrige award were Motorola, Westinghouse Electric, and Globe Metallurgical Company. Motorola has pushed its quality program to extremely high levels for its electronic pagers, for instance, where they have gained a dominant share in Japan. Motorola's quality program currently aims for a maximum defect rate of 3.4 parts per million with zero defects targeted for 1991.

Motorola started its program in 1981 because of fierce competition from Japan in the electronics field. It sent employees from all levels to the Phil Crosby Quality College in Florida and the Juran Institute in Connecticut. In general, its program is largely internally developed. According to the award citation, "Motorola has been recognized for its success in rediscovering the critical role of the customer in demanding perfection. The company's fundamental objective is total customer satisfaction through quality improvement. Its six sigma quality program sets a goal of only 3.4 defects per million. To achieve this Motorola made statistical technologies a part of every employee's job."

A second winner, Westinghouse Electric, entered its commercial nuclear fuel division headquartered in Monroeville, Pennsylvania. The company credits its success to getting employees involved and committed. Westinghouse launched its program by taking 500 employees from all levels to Japan to see results there. Managers told employees that quality failures were costing Westinghouse $150 million annually for white-collar rework and $60 million for blue-collar rework. The company also changed its quality orientation from using internal data to almost exclusively seeking out customer opinions. According to the Malcolm Baldrige citation,

> Now 99.999 percent of the division's nuclear fuel rod assemblies are flawless as ascertained by more than 60 measurements. First time through yields are 87 percent compared with 50 percent a few years ago. . . . The commitment to total quality for the commercial nuclear fuel division of Westinghouse Electric Corporation results from what its chairman terms a cultural change—that is, embracing quality as a way of life. The company developed a method to monitor continuously 60 key quality areas called pulse points from customer satisfaction to product performance.

The third company to be awarded was Globe Metallurgical Company of Beverly, Ohio, and Selma, Alabama. Globe Metallurgical was the winner in the small business category (fewer than 500 employees). Of special interest is that Globe was put up for sale in 1986 by its parents when the parent was being acquired by Cleveland Cliffs Iron Company. Eventually, Globe was acquired through a leveraged buyout led by Kenneth E. Leach, vice president of administration, who helped put the team together for the purchase. Globe started its quality program when it faced low-priced import competition. With help from the American Supplier Institute, it started a quality improvement program in which product from the furnaces is custom blended for each customer rather than general classes of products being sent wherever they fit best. Before the program, 40 percent of product had to be altered before shipment; this has been cut to 3 percent. Customer complaints are down 91 percent. According to its award citation, "Globe Metallurgical Incorporated, a small company of 210 employees, has become the lowest cost, highest quality producer of ferral alloys and silicon materials in the United States. The company attempts to monitor and quantify every factor that influences product quality, making extensive use of computer control systems that continually advise workers whether targets are met."

What is key here is that the Malcolm Baldrige National Quality Award does indeed help motivate U.S. companies to improve their total quality management. Although Mallory Controls has enjoyed an excellent reputation among its customers for its quality and reliability programs, efforts now being taken at Mallory will further improve that position, making it a formidable global competitor for the future.

As another example of how a company has added value through manufacturing, consider True Temper Sports, the largest supplier of golf shafts to the U.S. golf club industry. Through metallurgy and processing True Temper is able to customize a golf shaft to achieve certain desirable flex point characteristics depending on the type of club head to which the shaft is attached as well as the golf pro's need for stiffness, flex point, and other characteristics. Through manufacturing, True Temper is consistently able to produce golf shafts that meet its customers' requirements.

True Temper Sports provided value added to its product as well as launched a major brand recognition marketing program. Golfers know that each club in their set has a different loft. Furthermore because each club has a different length, it can have a different flex point or kick point where bending occurs in a shaft.

To make the flex point concept possible, True Temper applies sophisticated metallurgical and manufacturing technology. It has discovered a proprietary way to manufacture high-alloy steel shafts with a recessed section placed at a different point on each different length of shaft. This recessed section causes the shaft to flex at the point most appropriate for its length, thus improving the capacity of the club to do the job it is designed to do.

As a result of this added value manufacturing program, True Temper has become the market leader in golf shafts. Furthermore, in 1988, construction began on a 235-thousand-square-foot plant in South Carolina in order to respond to the increasing popularity of golf, both abroad and in the United States, where it is the fastest-growing participation sport, and to meet the increased demand for True Temper golf shafts.

Based on the technology developed for golf shafts, True Temper plans to expand its specialty tubing business to new areas such as light-weight, high-strength metal tubing for high-performance bicycles as well as military antennas and auto products. According to Ed VanDyke, True Temper Sports president, the new plant will increase True Temper's production capacity and boost the unit sufficiency through the use of improved manufacturing processes and computerized state-of-the-art equipment for heat treating tube drawing and welding. Certainly, True Temper is an example of a manufacturing company that has increased value through manufacturing.

In summary, changes in industry will be created by the manufacturing personnel of the future. As the October 1986 report of the National Science Foundation–sponsored research project conducted by Robert T. Lund, Stephen R. Rosenthal, and Tom Wachtell at Boston University states,

> The profound changes in manufacturing technology imply corresponding profound consequences for the manufacturing organization. Senior manufacturing management now face a twofold task. In addition to having much of the responsibility for design and selection decisions related to new highly sophisticated technology, senior manufacturing executives must also affect the changes in manufacturing organization procedure and policy that will insure smooth transitions and profitable operation. For many managers, this role involves the means that exceed their knowledge basis and the type of skills with which they are equipped . . . The achievement of the integrated manufacturing processes place new demand on those who plan design, procure and operate systems of production. Planning must be more strategic. Computer integrated manufacturing systems, supported by high capacity telecommunications networks, will be the dominant new manufacturing technology. Pervasive new manufacturing technologies will lead to greater flexibility, faster set up, decreased through put time and closer coupling between process steps and between manufacturing support functions. Computer aided design and engineering methods will provide faster design and design to manufacturing transition capabilities. These capabilities will encourage more rapid product changes, customizing and shorter product life cycles. ("The Manufacturing Executive for the 1990s," Boston: Boston University, Center for Technology and Policy.)

The BU report concludes that executives of the future must be able not only to recognize the benefits of change but also to anticipate negative consequences so that their adverse effects can be mitigated or avoided. Successful managers will employ strong leadership skills, understand technology and anticipate its implications, and create workable alternatives in advance of attempted change.

12

Real-Time Manufacturing Management: The Wave of the Future

Throughout this book, I have described at length the opportunities that lie within the factory's walls. And I have often criticized both plant managers and their corporate bosses because they don't make full use of those opportunities—or because they often don't even see them. As I have suggested, they have trouble seeing and seizing on these opportunities because *they look at the factory the wrong way.*

In a very real way, the factory today is really not a factory at all. Yes, it is a building in which actual products are manufactured, but the way in which those products are manufactured is radically different from what it used to be. Successfully managing the flow of work in a factory no longer relies on the smooth operation of mechanical machines but on the smooth flow of information. In this one fact lies the power of any American manufacturing plant to become a viable operation unto itself and an important part of its corporate parent's global strategy.

In the industrial age, a plant manager could obtain only an approximate and intuitive idea of what was going on in the factory and what problems arose on the shop floor, so they frequently solved a problem inefficiently. A generation ago, instead of keeping better track of stock, we hired stock chasers to search for whatever was needed at a particular time. Factories were not well integrated, at least by current standards, because information was not available to integrate them. We had to rely on manual systems and people to serve as the cogs.

Today factories have the ability to monitor everything that goes on in the factory very precisely—far more precisely, in fact, than any factory worker would have imagined just fifteen years ago. This has placed tremendous power in the hands of the plant manager and the people he works with. Each machine operator can check his own work rather than rely on quality control. Each customer can control the company's supply and scheduling network to serve his needs rather than rely on salespeople and production schedulers at the factory to do it. In essence, all these powers have made information the most important tool in the factory today. Understand the information and you understand the factory. Manipulate the information well, and you can run the factory well.

As we have seen, too often plant managers, under pressure from their corporate bosses, do not use the information well. They take bits and pieces of this information and put it to work, but they do not use its full power. Instead of rethinking a manufacturing process, they install an automated machine to perform the same old inefficient chores, only faster. They gather an amazing amount of information about what goes on inside the factory, but they do not use it to understand, in a systematic way, how to improve the factory's operation.

If the rest of the world had remained the same over the last thirty years, it might not matter that our best manufacturing corporations don't take full advantage of the opportunities technology provides. But the rest of the world has not remained the same. U.S. manufacturing faces fierce competition from everywhere else in the world. We *must* work smarter. And that means we must take advantage of every opportunity presented to us. If we recognize our opportunities and use them, we will survive cheap Asian labor, currency fluctuations, and the awesome commitment of the Japanese and Korean work forces.

That means that both the corporate bosses and the plant managers must change and learn to take advantage of every opportunity. And to do that, they must begin to *view the factory in a different way.* Corporate management has to understand the strategic importance of manufacturing. They must understand that a new manufacturing process—or a more efficient way of running orders through the factory or a work force with multiple diagnostic skills—can be just as helpful as laying off people or moving to Asia. Plant managers must recognize the opportunities that lie within the walls of their own factories.

Though it takes a lot of hard work, it isn't difficult to recognize the kinds of commonsense approaches needed to be made by U.S. factories. All that's required, on the part of both corporate executives and plant managers, is an ability to cast off the prejudices of the past and see manufacturing today for what it truly is: an area with tremendous and even exciting opportunities for workers to do meaningful tasks, for automation and information processing to bring powerful new efficiencies to bear on manufacturing processes, and for U.S. corporations to devise new strategies of staying competitive. But common sense means, above all, identifying and taking advantage of every opportunity—because only by taking full advantage of the factory of opportunity will we be able to compete.

The End—or the Beginning?

On Thursday, February 27, 1989, two well-dressed businessmen drove into the parking lot of the Farmington, Connecticut, base of Emhart Corporation, a $2.7 billion global company. At precisely 4:28 P.M. they walked into Emhart's corporate headquarters and asked the receptionist to meet with Morgan Hussey, Emhart's corporate secretary. The two gentlemen, briefcases in hand, were asked if they had an appointment, to which they replied in the negative. When asked the purpose of their visit, they simply replied that "They were here to buy Emhart."

At 4:30 P.M. the Dow Jones tape announced that Topper had just made a $35 tender offer for Emhart. My office at Emhart was next to Gil O'Niel, the corporate vice president of investor relations. Within seconds after the Dow Jones tape announcement, all telephones in our vicinity began to ring unceasingly—phone call after phone call after phone call. Newspapers, financial analysts, institutional investors, individual investors, Channels 3, 8, and 30, Dow Jones—all hit their telephones as soon as they saw the announcement. In the lobby, the two gentlemen presented Morgan Hussey with detailed papers covering the tender offer from Topper for Emhart.

While phones continued to ring outside our offices, Kathy Deniega, Emhart's PR administrator, began a series of calls to find out who Topper was. Simultaneously, my secretary, Claire DeJoseph, and O'Niel's secretary, Kathy Simcik, were answering phones. O'Niel also went from phone to phone giving one message: "We have just learned about the tender offer, and at this time Emhart has no statement until management has had sufficient time to study the offer."

At 4:45 Kathy Deniega handed a piece of paper to O'Niel as he explained to a financial analyst that Emhart also was surprised by the offer. Kathy's note read, "Topper, an organization formed for the acquisition of Emhart, in which the principals are the Fisher brothers representing a real estate group in New York and Gordon Getty, the son of J. Paul Getty."

The telephone calls waned, and the next day Emhart became the most active stock on the New York Stock Exchange. All of us at the corporate office realized something that affected the company, its employees, and ultimately, the state for the next three months: Topper had just put Emhart into play.

The events of the next few months were unlike any I have experienced in my entire business career. Once Topper made the offer, the corporate offices were never again the same. The company was never the same. In fact, Emhart is no more.

Immediately following the Topper offer, Peter Scott, Emhart's chairman, president, and chief executive officer, mustered his financial and legal executives in New York and brought in Wasserstein and Perella, and Shearson Lehman Hutton, Inc. as the company's financial advisors. Their objective was to develop a strategy and response to the Topper bid.

The rest of the officers became sounding boards for rumors. Each new rumor brought someone to any available officer, trying to explore whether there was any truth to the rumor. The more we denied the rumors, the more the employees did not believe that we did not know what was going on. In fact, throughout this period, most of the officers at Emhart were also listening to rumors because only a handful of executives associated with the financial and legal departments understood the events that were taking place.

Much happened in the two months following the offer. Initially, Emhart's board of directors recommended to stockholders that they reject Topper's $35-per-share bid. This recommendation was followed by a white-knight bid of $40 from Black and Decker.

Allegations of greenmail and stock parking peppered the news media. On the various business television channels, new rumors surfaced almost daily: A Japanese company was bidding for Emhart. An English company was accumulating stock. A leveraged buyout was being considered. Management was considering buying the company. The company would restructure. The company would recapitalize.

In the end, it was Black and Decker, with its $40 bid, that acquired Emhart. A few of the other officers at Emhart will go with Black and Decker; others are seeking new opportunities.

As I reached the end of my career at Emhart, I resigned my position as vice president of technology for the Emhart Corporation on May 31, 1989. I plan to launch a new career as a member of the faculty at the University of Connecticut. At UCONN I will be starting new courses in the management of technology, working with the School of Engineering and the School of Business to explore technology in the nineties. I intend to create courses that capitalize on the experiences I have had and also the experiences that companies I've been associated with have had, pointing the way for managing technology in the next decade. I intend to tell it like it is and assist students in achieving successful careers in managing technology.

As for the Black and Decker move—well, the jury is still out. It has a $2.8 billion debt to service, but its consumer marketing base has been strengthened with the addition of Emhart's consumer business. It also has a new market opportunity through Emhart's diversified industrial business. How this all will be put together will be resolved in the near future, I am sure. I now move on to teach students about technology opportunities based on my experiences in a rewarding technical management career as physicist, engineer, manager, and executive.

Appendix

It All Starts with a Design

No single discipline—not automation, robotics, not even advanced technology—will play as large a role in determining the success or failure of manufacturing in the future as product design. The customer's perception of the product and its features started with product design. The cost to manufacture the product, the selling price to the customer, and the cost to service had their basis in product design.

Whatever is produced on the factory floor starts with an engineering drawing traditionally produced from a blueprint, increasingly being made from a computer-generated drawing, and eventually to be produced from electronic impulses bypassing the traditional drafting process.

Whatever the profit to the company, the value to the customer and the performance and useful life of the product started when an engineer put a line on a piece of paper or keyed in a computer-aided design terminal. Materials used in the product, the manufacturing process ultimately used to make the product, and the shop-floor experiences that occurred have their roots in how well the engineer designed the product for manufacture.

Most important, to take maximum advantage of factory automation and to effectively use the advanced technologies that will emerge in the future, companies need to implement a design-for-manufacturing awareness as the first step in revitalizing their manufacturing competitiveness. DFM (design for manufacturing) must become a way of life within a company's engineering and manufacturing functions. DFM is essentially a culture-shaping process within a company. Nowhere in the company is the need for a closer relationship more acute than between engineering (those responsible for designing a product) and manufacturing (those responsible for making a product).

Beyond "Over the Wall"

For years design and manufacturing have operated in their own separate domains within companies, communicating infrequently during the early stages of a product design—if at all. Traditionally, the design process has been described as a product being thrown "over the wall."

Unfortunately, the wall—real or imaginary—separates design engineering and manufacturing by culture. Moreover, whether the two departments are on different floors, in separate buildings, cities, or countries, or even within the same office, a culture barrier separates those who design a product and those who manufacture that product.

Traditionally, product design is associated with translating customer functional requirements, usually specified by marketing departments, into physical design parameters. Design is thought of as the process that transforms the functional description of a product into a physical entity. Within this cultural framework, a sequential approach to product development has become the traditional way that products are developed, designed, and manufactured within a company.

Significantly, during very early product development stages, R&D and engineering personnel are more concerned with how a feature specified by marketing can be translated into a physical parameter and not how a design is produced or whether the design meets cost targets. Furthermore, cost targets are often missing or specified in some ambiguous manner—"design to the lowest cost" often being the traditional design cost specification.

On occasion manufacturing personnel are consulted by product designers, but this was often an informal communication link generally associated with the procurement of long-lead tooling. Herein lies another traditional culture barrier. Manufacturing engineers are primarily concerned with tooling, while product engineers view their design as performance oriented. Design and manufacturing engineers look at a product design from different viewpoints. Moreover, within the cultural framework the manufacturing engineer is isolated from the conceptual phase of a product design—intentionally or unintentionally—while the design engineer is isolated from the tooling aspects of producing the product. Moreover, two sets of drawings often are prepared—namely, the design prints by product engineers and tooling drawings by manufacturing engineers—which adds to the cultural barrier.

Even after the release of engineering designs into a factory, the cultural separation of the two functions continues. Designers simply believe that their job is finished when their drawings are released. At that point the designs disappear into the manufacturing engineers' domain, and they struggle to build products that are "dumped into their laps."

Many companies now have come to recognize the disadvantages of the sequential product development approach and the pitfalls of the barrier culture that isolates design and manufacturing. Managers now realize that traditional sequential approaches and isolated cultures are responsible for extended development times that force many companies to miss market opportunities. It is now being recognized that the isolation of manufacturing during the early stages of a product design often results in numerous engineering changes after products have been released for manufacture or even after longer periods after field experiences with customers reveal further manufacturing problems.

This appendix identifies how to effectively bring together the design and manufacturing functions. It explores various concepts and techniques now being implemented by many companies that have come to realize that design and manufacturing are two separate functions that can be culturally drawn together to work more effectively.

Removing the Barrier

Thirty-five engineers and manufacturing personnel assembled in a motel conference room in Amherst, Massachusetts, to attend a seminar conducted by Geofrey Boothroyd, former professor from the University of Massachusetts and now with the University of Rhode Island. Boothroyd is known internationally for the course in design for assembly that he developed with P. Dewhurst while both were at UMass.

The group in Amherst, Massachusetts, represented engineering and manufacturing personnel from Emhart's global hardware business. Representatives attended the meeting from Kwikset in Anaheim, California, Russwin-Corbin commercial hardware in Berlin, Connecticut, DOM in West Germany, and VSB in Appledorn, Holland. The products manufactured and marketed by these market leaders consisted of door locks, deadbolts, and door closures.

Significantly, the problem confronting Emhart's hardware business was becoming quite evident in the eighties. Unfortunately, the solutions were complex.

In the eighties Asian imports began to make significant inroads against Emhart's traditional hardware business. What used to be the shelf space domain of Kwikset in hardware stores, discount stores, and DIY centers was challenged by imports from Taiwan, Korea, and Hong Kong. Furthermore, Emhart's commercial hardware products also were being attacked from suppliers that were locating in low-cost labor areas.

Emhart, with factories in New Britain, Connecticut, Anaheim, California, and Bristol, Oklahoma, responded to the Asian threat with major cost-reduction programs and a significant move toward automation. Its marketing department launched advertising campaigns, working closely with law enforcement agencies to help convince consumers of the merits of Kwikset deadbolts. Discounts, point-of-sale promotions, giveaways—all stops were pulled as Emhart fought to keep its dominant position in the door hardware business.

In the midst of this competitive battle we learned an important lesson. As Emhart's hardware divisions automated, anticipated gains through automation were not achieved. When analyzing the reasons for these disappointing results, we discovered that many of the divisions were merely applying mechanistic techniques to their existing locks. No attempts were being made to reexamine existing lock designs. Some locks had over fifty parts, and these parts often differed from product to product, although the products had similar functions.

As parts proliferated and performance levels remained lower than expected, Fred Hollfelder, Emhart's general manager for the Hardware Division, recognized that automating an existing product line without redesigning the product was not taking full advantage of technology's promise. To help create the needed change in his division, Hollfelder brought together his engineering and manufacturing team to attend Boothroyd's UMass design seminar. Boothroyd, a pioneer of design for automation, had developed a system for identifying and classifying the degree of difficulty for a specific design in either a manual assembly mode or through automation.

Through a week-long session, hardware engineers and manufacturing personnel together applied Boothroyd's principles for arriving at "figures of merit" for their existing hardware designs. In all cases the system developed by Boothroyd illustrated the degree of difficulty that was being encountered as automation was applied at the factory to existing door hardware designs. Furthermore, the Boothroyd analysis illustrated that even manual assembly of these products would be difficult because of the characteristics and large number of parts used in Emhart's traditional product lines.

The seminar attendees left the week-long session convinced that unless their products were designed for automation, they would not be taking full advantage of automation principles. As a result, significant gains were made throughout Emhart's Hardware Division as product engineers and manufacturing personnel applied the design for automation principles learned from their Boothroyd experience.

For me, the Emhart experience was not new. While at the Singer Company I encountered the same situations with sewing machines. As new fabric materials came on the market and as Singer's marketing organization specified additional features, the parts used in a sewing machine proliferated to great numbers: Singer's top-of-the-line machine contained well over 900 parts. Of concern, however, was that many of these parts were being redesigned and changed every time a new machine was introduced into the marketplace. Until we applied design-for-automation principles, automated assembly of these machines did not result in the expected performance levels.

Another Japanese Story

On my trips to Japan I often noted that Japanese factories' automation cells generally had a display board of parts that were being assembled at each station. The boards indicated that very few parts were being assembled at each of the automation cells. For products similar to hardware locks, no more than six to ten parts were being assembled at each station, and the majority of stations had only six or seven parts. From station to station there was a similarity of parts on each board, and it was not unusual to see two or three of the same parts at several assembly stations.

The lesson to learn from the Japanese is that when they automate a product, they group assemblies into individual cells. Significantly, each automation cell unit assembles as few parts as possible, and many of the same parts are being used throughout all of the automation cells.

These are very simple commonsense rules, yet many designers will develop an automation system for assembling more than fifteen or twenty parts rather than consider the automation of smaller subassemblies and then finally assembling these subsystems.

Also, using similar parts throughout the design process is not practiced by engineers to the extent that it should be throughout U.S. companies. It is my belief that significant gains could be made in many companies if managers were to implement techniques for ensuring that product designs do indeed take advantage of similar parts throughout a manufacturing operation.

Ask the Right Questions

The discipline of using similar parts throughout the design process requires continual pressure from engineering management. While I was director of productivity for Emhart, I sent questionnaires to each of our manufacturing operations. In this questionnaire, I simply asked the operational vice presidents to identify how many new parts were being designed for each new product as well as specific questions related to the proliferation of these new parts. One of the questions, for example, was to identify how many different fasteners were being used in each of their products. Surprising answers came back from our industrial machine operations: Well over 100 different fasteners were being used within the same product. Also, parts were dramatically increasing with each design.

Our parts analysis showed us that engineers often design a product without considering whether similar parts exist within their manufacturing organization. As a result, many manufacturing units continue a proliferation of parts. Each time a new part enters a factory, a series of events takes place. Not only is there a need for developing and manufacturing that particular part, but there is also a need to track the part, to inventory the part, and to ensure that the part is catalogued for servicing and spare parts. All of this adds to the cost and to the complexities that occur in today's factories.

From my experience, less than 20 percent of the parts thought to require new designs are actually needed. Of the remaining new parts, 40 percent could be obtained from an existing design, while the other 40 percent could be created by modifying an existing part. This experience is verified over and over again whether the product is a sewing machine, a door lock, a consumer product such as a glue gun, or a complex industrial product such as a high-speed automated electronic chip placement machine for automated circuit board production. Ask the question in your company, and you will learn that all too often new parts are being designed for each product without exploring whether parts that already exist can be used or possibly modified slightly, hence reducing total parts count in a factory and subsequently reducing cost and the operational complexities associated with adding these new parts.

While the reduction of parts through product design produces significant improvements in a manufacturing operation, design for manufacturing techniques produces even greater gains. For this reason, it is essential that technical managers in both engineering and manufacturing implement techniques that improve the design-for-manufacturing process. In the remainder of this appendix I review some major approaches to the DFM process.

Implement DFM in Your Company

All products can benefit from a program that emphasizes and utilizes techniques to ensure that design for manufacturing is being considered by product designers. The company gains a more effective design and manufacturing interface, reduces the product development time to market, and also ensures fewer engineering changes when the product hits the factory floor. Furthermore, experience shows that an effective DFM strategy also increases the reliability of products.

There are many DFM concepts, and in this appendix I have selected the following as those I highly recommend for consideration by technical managers: design reviews, group technology, the Taguchi method, design for assembly, value engineering, and design axioms.

Design Reviews

The term *design review* is used throughout companies and industry to describe a formal process that assists managers and individual contributors in evaluating product designs with the objective of making improvements that are appropriate to the design assurance needs of a business. The design review is a formal independent evaluation of a product design through persons other than those directly responsible and accountable for the design. Its primary purpose is to confirm that the product design as planned or completed is likely to or does in fact meet all product objectives and manufacturing requirements, as well as to ensure that the product will satisfactorily perform with the customer.

Informal design reviews in some form or another do take place as a regular activity in most engineering functions. Designers often obtain counsel from their peers in informal sessions, technical managers review the work of their subordinates, and engineers meet informally with individuals from other functions to discuss design plans or problems. In all these reviews, whether formal or informal, an interaction does take place and contributes to improved design. However, I have noted through many years of managing technology that there is a need for formal milestone reviews, at which time all functions associated with the product development process can have an opportunity to discuss the process. Furthermore, bringing in outside expertise can ensure that a design has been properly critiqued from all aspects.

The formal design review is the mechanism for understanding the problems that will be encountered with a new product development program—whether those problems are associated with the actual design of the product, the manufacturing of the product, the final cost, or the field and service experiences associated with the product when it reaches the marketplace.

A formal design review may uncover areas of uncertainty and potential risk and alternate design approaches or topics for further study. Because design reviews are independent evaluations of a product design by qualified persons other than those directly responsible and accountable for the design, they provide an added measure of assurance that the design will fulfill its requirement.

Design reviews are preplanned, scheduled, and conducted at key milestone periods during the product development process. Although an informal network exists within engineering and manufacturing activities, a formal design review program results in significant contributions to design adequacy and manufacturability that are difficult to achieve by the informal performance characteristics of the operating design process.

Four major contributions can be attributed to a formalized design review process—namely, a concentration of additional technical knowledge, interactive guidance from other functions from within the company, experience and judgment not readily available on a day-to-day basis, and evaluation by qualified people who can view it from a new perspective. People who are not steeped in the thinking of the design team or committed to any approach can be more objective about the pros and cons of a project and more candid about its potential risks and uncertainties. Moreover, the design review stimulates the design team to "put its thinking in order." The process of preparing for the design review and the mere act of describing the logic of the design approach to another team of technically qualified personnel unfamiliar with the design cause the design team to sharpen its perspective and thinking on the logic and approach. Most important, the design review is a formal opportunity for the design team to stand back, reflect, and take a fundamental look at the overall design—something they may not have had the opportunity to do under the daily pressure of a design effort.

A design review is a nonthreatening, constructive, creative discussion among peers who encourage probing and searching—by reviewers and designers alike. The review can be more fundamental and go to greater depths than is generally the case in a review involving responsible designers and their managers alone. The results are a synergistic interaction between the review team and the design team that produces perspectives, ideas, and alternatives that may not have developed otherwise. It is a growth experience for all participants.

Specific techniques seem to be inherent in all effective design review systems. Techniques may vary from company to company, but the following are frequently present in successful design reviews.

1. Design reviews must be backed by a management policy that defines the type of reviews to be held, sets the schedule for such reviews, assigns responsibilities for conducting the reviews, and allows for the resources necessary to carry out the review.
2. The design review must be planned in advance and occur prior to key events or major design decision points.
3. The starting point for design review is a clear statement of design objectives and requirements, usually in the form of a design specification. (It is interesting to note that in the majority of design reviews in which I have participated, the design specification is either often lacking or incomplete. In

fact, conducting the design review usually reveals that such specifications are indeed missing.)

4. The design reviews are to be conducted by competent professionals who have the respect of the design team.
5. The design review is *not* a show-and-tell exercise. Sufficient time must be provided for the review team to question and probe.
6. The review is performed in a cooperative environment where designers and reviewers mutually strive for agreement on design and actions. In a sense, a design review is a license to critique. When properly conducted, the not-invented-here syndrome is guarded against. All attendees are made aware that a critique is the nature of the review.
7. The design review reviews the design and not the designer.
8. The design review process should provide for a formal procedure for acting on or rejecting review team recommendations. That is, there should be a recording of the results of the design review, assignment of action responsibilities, time limits, follow-up, and formal management review and approval.

Many decisions are made throughout the design process, but there usually are certain milestones at which reviews may be appropriate. From my experience, three general design reviews are applicable to most design needs:

1. *The concept review.* This design review is held in the advanced development or proposal stage prior to commitment to a final design approach primarily to ensure that the design specifications meet quality objectives and requirements and that the design concept will fulfill the specification in the best known way.
2. *The early design review.* This review is held during the early part of a design phase when layouts and schematics are available in order to evaluate the overall design approach, design implementation plan, design analysis and early test results, design margins, materials application, and manufacturability.
3. *Design release review.* This review is conducted to critique the overall readiness for production prior to release of drawings

to manufacturing where a review of all of the technical disciplines is conducted along with prototype test results.

The early design review should cover such areas as whether the product uses a technology with which a company's manufacturing operation has design application or operational experience. Will a new material be used? Are new manufacturing processes or advanced production techniques required for critical components? Even if the product technology is basically unchanged, does the design require significant changes beyond those that a particular manufacturing organization might have relative to the size of the equipment, power rating, or any other changes that manufacturing should know about?

The design review leader should be someone other than the designer or design program leader. Such practice allows designers to maximize their effort on the design itself and enhances the potential for a more objective review of the design and alternate design consideration.

The chairperson should set a climate in which it is evident that the review team is there to advise and help the design team by contributing its collective knowledge and experience. It must be evident that the design team retains full responsibility and accountability for the design but that the review will be successful only if the critical design issues are fully exposed and examined in a frank, open, and objective manner.

From my experience in conducting and attending many design reviews, there are certain key areas that consistently come up throughout each of these sessions. The following summary illustrates what can be accomplished by conducting a design review. In general, these problems consistently come up in design reviews:

1. The initial set of specifications are either missing or incomplete or contain ambiguous areas subject to interpretation that can lead to problems as the project proceeds.
2. Manufacturing generally is not represented in the early de-

sign reviews or even in the second major milestone design review. (From my experience, manufacturing needs to be involved in the very early stages of the design review process.)

3. Cost targets are lacking or ambiguous. In some cases, a simple statement such as "Design at the lowest possible cost" is considered to be the cost target, leading to a great deal of misunderstanding on the part of the marketing organization, the engineers and manufacturing. (I strongly recommend that a cost target be established and reviewed during the initial design review as well as updated in subsequent reviews in the design review process.)

4. Design reviews can turn into design presentations that don't permit reviewers to ask questions and discuss alternatives. (From my experience, not more than 25 percent of the total review time should be used in presentation of the design and related material. The other 75 percent should be used for asking questions and discussing alternatives.)

5. No one officially takes notes. (The secretary or recorder's only purpose should be to keep accurate minutes of the proceedings, including accurate delineation of all problems, comments, recommendations, and action items discussed at the review.)

6. No follow-up occurs. (A form can be prepared that facilitates postmeeting response. For example, the form might include a design evaluation where each review member gives an overall evaluation of the discipline for which they are a member of the review board. The rating must be in terms of the customer specification, performance or design requirements, and company design practices. This form also would list potential problem areas based on review board members experiences with similar designs. A recommendation section would provide for suggested improvements in the design that become action items. Finally, a general comments section can offer review board members an opportunity to provide miscellaneous comments such as administration of the review, methods of design presentation, omissions, or a minority opinion.)

7. No final report is written. (A final report of the design review should be prepared by the review chairperson and

include the following: recommendations of review team members with actions decided at the review meeting, generally included in minutes; planned disposition or response to recommendations not resolved at a review meeting; recommendation of review team members submitted after the review meeting. The final report should indicate the responsibility and schedule for taking all the necessary action that resulted from the review. Copies of the minutes and the final report should go to all who were part of the review plus others who will be directly affected by the results.)

Group Technology

In a manufacturing operation, when are two parts similar? Most people would say that two parts are similar when they look alike. Two parts that look alike may not be considered similar from a manufacturing viewpoint, however. If one of the parts that are similar in appearance requires a different manufacturing process, then from a manufacturing viewpoint the two parts are not normally be considered similar.

In manufacturing, similarity refers to parts that are made by similar machining processes. In a factory, metal parts are made by a sequence of operations including cutting, boring, milling, grinding, and turning on a lathe. Thus, the same set of machine tools can often make a great variety of parts, from gun barrels to cam shafts.

By grouping parts in accordance with the production processes used on each part, manufacturing operations can be grouped in a cell fashion such that parts similar by processing standards can be produced in a complete cell even though the parts do not look similar. This is the basis of group technology. GT is an approach to design and manufacture that seeks to reduce manufacturing systems information content by identifying and exploiting the sameness or similarity of parts based on their geometrical shape or similarities in their production process. Parts that appear the same can be grouped according to group technology principles, but the main advantage of the group technology concept is to group together parts that will be processed in a similar fashion.

In using GT the designers use classification and coding systems to identify and understand part similarities and to establish the processing actions required for the parts. As a DFM tool, group technology can be used in a variety of ways to produce significant design efficiency and product performance and quality improvements.

One rapidly effective approach is to use GT to facilitate significant reductions in design time and effort. In using a GT system, the design engineer needs only to identify the code that describes the desired part. A search of the GT data base reveals whether a similar part already exists. If a similar part is found to exist, and this is most often the case, the designer can simply modify the existing design to accommodate the new part.

Group technology also can be used effectively to help control parts proliferation occurring in most factories and to eliminate redundant part designs by facilitating standardization and rationalization approaches. If not controlled, parts proliferation can reach epidemic proportions, especially in large companies that manufacture many different products and product models. By noting similarities between parts, it is often possible to create standardized parts that can be used interchangeably in a variety of applications and products.

The Taguchi Method

The Taguchi method is a quality-oriented concept initiated by Dr. Genichi Taguchi, executive director of the American Supplier Institute Incorporated of Dearborn, Michigan, and a winner of the 1986 Rockwell Medal for excellence in technology as well as four Deming prizes. Taguchi's approach combines engineering and statistical methods to achieve improvements in cost and quality by optimizing product design and manufacturing processes. Taguchi's engineering concepts regarding product and process quality are twofold: (1) Quality must be designed into products and processes; it cannot be achieved with inspection, tests, or product screening; (2) conformance to specifications is not good enough; as soon as product parameters deviate from the nominal dimension, losses from poor quality will multiply.

A key factor in Taguchi's method is the emphasis on cross-functional team interaction. In applying Taguchi methods, design engineers and manufacturing engineers learn to talk to each other in a common language. Through this method, design and manufacturing engineers pinpoint which variables have the strongest functional relationship to the product requirements. The Taguchi method also isolates the effects on the product of adjusting controllable manufacturing variables and determines the effect of the uncontrollable variations on the manufacturing process and on quality.

The Taguchi method achieves its results through the application of experimental designs using statistical tools called an orthoganal array. Using these orthoganal arrays yields an approach to planned experimentation.

It is noted, however, that engineers using Taguchi methods report mixed results, especially relative to the complexity of the statistical concepts. As Paul Schmidt, manufacturing engineer at McSwain Manufacturing Company of Cincinnati, reports in the May 1987 issue of *Manufacturing Engineering* (an SME publication), "The Taguchi methods were easier to learn than anticipated and the cost associated with conducting the experimental design was minimal."

On the other hand, Douglas Montgomery of Arizona State University in an article in the September 1988 *Manufacturing Engineering* states, "Taguchi's engineering concepts are excellent and should be adopted by all companies that are interested in improving the quality of their products and reducing their development costs. However, his statistical concepts are somewhat cumbersome and inefficient and can be replaced by simpler techniques." Most of Taguchi's experimental design techniques are based on the factorial design concept. In comparison to the one-factor-at-a-time approach and other methods commonly used by development engineers with no knowledge of experimental design, anything that is based on the factorial principle, no matter how inefficient, will produce better results.

From my experience, the Taguchi method overcomes many practices traditionally associated with experimental testing throughout most engineering organizations. In general, the traditional approach is to deal with a variable on a single basis—that is, to change the experiment one variable at a time. On occasion tests will be conducted changing a few variables. Yet the real world is multivariant.

Unless experiments can be designed to consider a multitude of variables and to identify the critical variations and their effect on the total test, the experiment is not truly representative of what a product or process encounters in real-world practical situations.

The Taguchi method addresses the issue of multiple variables. Even though the method is considered complex, product engineers and manufacturing engineers will need to develop the degree of statistical sophistication necessary to design experiments that can have a significant impact on product and process development and the improvements needed in quality of both aspects.

Design for Assembly

Among the best-known design-for-assembly systems are Boothroyd and Dewhurst's design for assembly, described in their book *Design for Assembly: A Designer's Handbook* (Boothroyd, Dewhurst Incorporated, Wakefield, Rhode Island). A similar approach developed for General Electric by Hitachi also uses these concepts.

These and other systems calculate a score for a product based on the number of its parts, the simplicity of the parts, and how these parts function during assembly—either manual assembly or automation. Design-for-assembly techniques developed by Boothroyd and Dewhurst emphasize minimizing the number of parts and assigning numerical values to different methods of putting things together. This enables an engineer to measure how efficient a design is from an assembly standpoint.

As noted in the introductory section of this appendix, the concepts of design for assembly by Boothroyd were used extensively throughout Emhart's hardware group. Excellent results were obtained by using Boothroyd's design-for-assembly system to address an area of product design in manufacturing that was not considered as thoroughly as it should have been in the early stages of a product design.

After studying Boothroyd's design for automation concepts, one observes that the principles that he espouses are really the application of common sense to product design. His recommends avoiding projections, holes, or slots that will cause tangling when identical parts are placed in a parts feeder. The system also gives higher marks to parts that are designed symmetrical to avoid the need for extra orienting devices and the corresponding loss in feeder efficiency. When symmetry cannot be achieved, Boothroyd recommends developing designs that incorporate means to facilitate orientation.

From my experience, the design-for-automation principles as developed by Boothroyd and Dewhurst are necessary for every engineering manager. Applying these techniques can produce significant improvements in product design and manufacturing in a wide variety of products.

Value Engineering

Value engineering, also called value analysis, is a systematic approach to evaluating design alternatives. This method seeks creative ways to eliminate unnecessary features and functions and to achieve required performance at the lowest possible cost while optimizing manufacturability, quality, and delivery.

The technique of value engineering uses multidisciplinary teams to analyze the functions divided by a product design and determines the cost of each function. In conducting the analysis, attention is devoted to the value that is achieved by a product function.

According to value engineering principles, every component in a product contributes both to the cost and the performance of the entire system. Thus, by analyzing the ratio of performance to the cost of each component, the relative values can be obtained for individual components. Obtaining the maximum performance per unit cost is the basic objective of value engineering.

Like design reviews, I consider value engineering essential to managing a technical function. The value engineering discipline is certainly not new. Nevertheless, value engineering concepts and methods are very effective in identifying the essential characteristics of a product design. Through the technique a comparison of value ratios enables one to evaluate alternative designs along with the implications that these designs have on cost and manufacturability.

Recently, computer disks have been generated for conducting value engineering programs. I have heard negative comments about such computer programs by traditional value analysis experts who proclaim that their method is a simple procedure and hence can be performed without computer aids. In my opinion, such computer programs are helpful and should be encouraged. These programs provide an orderly disciplined method by which a value-engineering analysis can be conducted. Granted, those in value engineering are very familiar with the techniques, but most engineers in engineering functions and manufacturing engineering have not been exposed to the disciplines of value engineering. Computer programs are an excellent tool for taking these engineers through a value engineering program.

Design Axioms

An axiomatic approach to design is based on the belief that fundamental principles of axioms of good design exist and that the use of those axioms to guide and evaluate design decisions leads to good designs. By definition, an axiom must be applicable to the full range of design decisions and to all stages, phases, and levels of the design process.

A pioneer in the field of design axioms is Professor Nam P. Suh, former NSF assistant director for engineering and now a professor at MIT. According to Nam Suh,

> One of the major problems of the manufacturing field has been that we rely too much on empiricism in all aspects of operation, be it the design of the product, design of the process, or the operation of the manufacturing system. The common problem with an empiricism-dominated field is that the existing knowledge cannot be stated in a generalizable form, or transmitted to others in an effective way without requiring the accumulation of a similar experience base. If we are to make the field of manufacturing into a discipline, we need to establish the science base.

Nam Suh claims that we can treat the design and synthesis process scientifically using what he calls design axioms. *Axioms* by his definition are absolute principles that are required in making rational design decisions for products, processes, systems, and software.

From my experience and discussions with Nam Suh, I believe that his design axioms approach as applied to product design in manufacturing has considerable merit. Unfortunately, like many new concepts, there is a perception that the method is complex. As a result of his efforts with many companies using the principles, however, simplified approaches have been developed. Almost all engineering design groups and manufacturing engineers will find the concept easy to use and capable of making significant improvements in the product design and manufacturing process as more experience is gained through the application of axiomatics to practical problems.

Nam Suh's approach clarifies a very important step in product design—namely, to define a set of functional requirements in what he calls the functional domain that satisfy the perceived needs for a product or a process. His second step is then to create a physical being in the physical domain that satisfies the stated functional requirements.

According to Suh, the design process involves transformation from the functional domain to the physical domain. In this sense, design can be defined as the process to transform the functional description of a product into a physical entity. The designer specifies how the transformation occurs by specifying the design parameters, the geometric shape, the physical component, the process, and the spatial and temporal relationship among them. The designer thus creates a set of information in the form of drawings, circuits, software, and equations that describe the transformation process.

It has been my experience that the whole area of transforming the functional requirements of a product into the physical design is not clearly understood by those who are associated with the design process, including marketing personnel, engineers, and manufacturing. One objective of Nam Suh in his work at MIT is to better understand functional specifications in order that marketing personnel and engineers can better understand the tradeoffs and the impact of developing and designing the parameters to achieve specific functional specs.

I believe Nam Suh's work to be a pioneering effort in what ultimately will develop into a design and manufacturing science as applied to the product design discipline. Nam Suh has stated the objectives of his design axiomatic program on numerous occasions at conferences held on the subject. According to Nam Suh, "The maximum increase in manufacturing productivity will be possible when high value added products are made using efficient manufacturing technologies." He further states "that the rational design of products and processes cannot be achieved through ad hoc approaches. Rather, we need to establish the science base for the manufacturing field." Finally, Nam Suh's major objective is to make manufacturing a discipline. In order to achieve this goal, he is devoting considerable effort to his axiomatic approach, which I heartily recommend to all engineering managers as a forerunner of a design discipline for the future.

Index

About the Author

John S. Rydz is visiting professor at the University of Connecticut, where he is developing and teaching courses in the management of technology. He is the former corporate vice president of technology for Emhart Corporation, a $2.7 billion multinational diversified corporation. As vice president of technology, he was responsible for developing worldwide technical strategies and fostering emerging technologies for Emhart's products and processes.

Prior to joining Emhart, Mr. Rydz was vice president and chief technical officer for the Sewing Products Group of the Singer Company. At Singer he developed the Athena 2000, the first electronic sewing machine. Mr. Rydz also directed Singer's worldwide technical activities, including R&D, product design, and manufacturing engineering.

Prior to joining Singer, he was corporate vice president at Diebold Incorporated, Canton, Ohio. During his five years there he pioneered Diebold's automated teller machines (ATMs) and helped take Diebold into electronic systems for the bank and finance markets.

Before joining Diebold, Mr. Rydz was research manager for Addressograph/Multigraph (now called AM International) in Cleveland, Ohio. At AM, he directed programs launching AM into plastic credit cards and credit card systems.

Prior to AM, Mr. Rydz was executive vice president and a director of Nuclear Corporation of America. Nucor was launched as a high-tech venture with financial support from The Martin Company and Bear Stearns, two Wall Street investment banks.

Mr. Rydz started his business career with the Radio Corporation of America where, for ten years, he held various management positions including manager of new business development and member of the corporate staff under RCA's senior executive vice president.

He is a graduate of the Massachusetts Institute of Technology with a B.S. in physics. He received his M.S. in physics from the University of Pennsylvania and has taken graduate business courses at Case Western Reserve.

Mr. Rydz is a past member of the National Science Foundation's Advisory Committee for Engineering. He has also served on the final selection committee for NSF's Engineering Research Center Program (ERCs).

He is a guest lecturer at MIT and Boston University and a member of MIT's Industrial Advisory Board on Manufacturing and Productivity, the University of Connecticut's School of Engineering Advisory Board (chairman), the University of Hartford's Engineering Executive Council, and Governor William A. O'Neill's Connecticut Technology Advisory Board.

Mr. Rydz holds several patents. He is a frequent lecturer and has written on a variety of subjects, including *Managing Innovation* (Ballinger).